Twayne's English Authors Series

EDITOR OF THIS VOLUME

Kinley Roby

Northeastern University

Charles Doughty

TEAS 298

Charles. M. Doughty.
1921

Charles Doughty

CHARLES DOUGHTY

By STEPHEN ELY TABACHNICK

Ben-Gurion University of the Negev

TWAYNE PUBLISHERS
A DIVISION OF G. K. HALL & CO., BOSTON

Published in 1981 by Twayne Publishers,
A Division of G. K. Hall & Co.
All Rights Reserved

Printed on permanent/durable acid-free paper and bound
in the United States of America

First Printing

Library of Congress Cataloging in Publication Data

Tabachnick, Stephen Ely.
Charles Doughty.

(Twayne's English authors series ; TEAS 298)
Bibliography: p. 173–77
Includes index.
1.   Doughty, Charles Montagu, 1843-1926—
Criticism and interpretation.
PR6007.085Z85   1981   821'.912   80-27178
ISBN 0-8057-6790-8

To Sharona and Daphne,
this

Contents

About the Author

S. E. Tabachnick is currently Associate Professor in the Department of Foreign Literatures, Ben-Gurion University of the Negev, Israel, where he specializes in the literature of British imperialism, particularly Anglo-Arabian travel writing. Dr. Tabachnick's publications include *T. E. Lawrence* (Twayne, 1978) and the coauthored *Harold Pinter* (1973), as well as numerous articles.

Preface

The problem faced by a critic of Doughty today is to determine which works of his have been justifiably and which unjustifiably neglected. Only two books on his art have ever appeared, and the most recent of these was written over forty years ago. Both are the products of unabashed partisans of the verse as well as the prose. My book presents a revision of this previous criticism from the viewpoint of our time and from the perspective of half a century of critical articles and dissertations.

Basically, I see *Travels in Arabia Deserta* as great primarily because it transcends Doughty's consciously held patriotic and religious prejudices, not because of them. I think the poetry—outside of *Adam Cast Forth*—weak because in it Doughty emphasizes rather than overcomes these prejudices and because it is poorly structured, frequently maudlin, and only occasionally stylistically vital. Only in *Arabia Deserta* and *Adam Cast Forth* does the artist in Doughty fully and successfully predominate over his narrow and rather unimaginative conscious mind.

The proportions of this book express concretely my appraisal of the relative merit of the works. The three long chapters which contain analyses of *Arabia Deserta*'s spiritual background, composition, personae, genre, and style, the major themes of the book, and the literary modes employed by Doughty to structure its major scenes, constitute the heart of my study. I seek to demonstrate that in spite of its marvelous uniqueness, Doughty's masterpiece makes more artistic sense and belongs closer to other late Victorian prose than had been previously believed. Two shorter chapters devoted to the major and minor poetry respectively rather mercilessly criticize flaws, but also praise more infrequent virtues—stylistic experimentation and fresh perceptions in the case of the major poetry, particularly *Adam Cast Forth*, and science-fictional, technological imagination in the minor works.

Since my view is in consonance with the majority opinion on Doughty developed since the last critical book on him was written, it is less than revolutionary. But I hope that I have managed to present honestly and objectively for our time the work of a writer whose one masterpiece has always inspired my profound admiration; and to inspire in my turn much-needed further study of its art and that of *Adam Cast Forth*, which deserves better than its present total neglect.

STEPHEN ELY TABACHNICK

Ben-Gurion University of the Negev

Acknowledgments

Mrs. Ruth M. Robbins, the librarians of the Fitzwilliam Museum and Gonville and Caius College, and the Syndics of Cambridge University, have kindly granted me permission to publish manuscript materials. Although our views of Doughty are quite different, Mrs. Robbins in conversation and letters has been very generous with her unrivaled knowledge of all aspects of his life and work. Francis Golffing, editor of *The Pre-Raphaelite Review*, allowed me to publish, in greatly revised form, my article listed in the bibliography; parts of chapters 2 and 3 are based on this article. The Letters of T. E. Lawrence Trust and Jonathan Cape Ltd. have given me permission to publish extracts from Lawrence's letters.

I am extremely grateful to Edwards Metcalf and especially to Dr. Philip O'Brien of Whittier College for unstinting bibliographical assistance of the highest order. I thank San Diego State University for the generous use of its facilities during 1978–1979 and Professors Maurice Friedman, Dan McLeod, William Rogers, Ita Sheres, and Don Shojai of its English and Comparative Literature Department, for making my sabbatical year enjoyable and intellectually stimulating. Among librarians at San Diego State, Valerie Edwards, Karen Hogarth, and Ann Wright of the interlibrary loan department served as my lifeline. And of course I thank the Ben-Gurion University, which provided me with a delightful year of research and writing.

Professor Kinley Roby has performed extremely useful editing. My wife Sharona supplied not merely moral support, but criticism, proofreading, and help with the index. As grateful as I am for all this aid, I must point out that all responsibility for any error of fact or interpretation is, unfortunately, my own. But I would use this opportunity to caution the reader that what looks like a typographical error may not be one: in addition to standard phonetic symbols, Doughty employs an unusual personal system of punctuation, and I have retained it in direct quotations wherever possible.

Chronology

1843   Charles Doughty born August 19 at Theberton Hall, Suffolk.

1856   Fails medical examination for Royal Navy.

1861– Attends Gonville and Caius College and Downing College,
1866   Cambridge, as student of geology.

1866   "On the Jöstedal-brae Glaciers in Norway" published.

1868– Reads early literature in Bodleian Library, Oxford.
1870

1871– Desultory travels in Europe, North Africa, and the Levant, cul-
1876   minating in year of Arabic studies in Damascus.

1876– 10 November–2 August, Arabian exploration.
1878

1884   Publication of *Documents épigraphiques recueillis dans le nord de l'Arabie* by the Paris Académie des Inscriptions et Belles Lettres.

1886   Marries Caroline McMurdo.

1888   Cambridge University Press publishes *Travels in Arabia Deserta*.

1892   Daughter Dorothy born.

1894   Daughter Freda born.

1900   Privately publishes *Under Arms 1900*.

1906– *The Dawn in Britain*.
1907

1908   *Adam Cast Forth*. Receives honorary D.Litt. from Oxford University.

1909   *The Cliffs*.

1912   *The Clouds*. Receives Royal Geographical Society's Gold Medal for his Arabian travels.

1916   *The Titans*.

1920   *Mansoul. Honoris Causa* conferred by Cambridge University.

1922   Made an Honorary Fellow of the British Academy.

1923   Revised version of *Mansoul* appears.

1926   20 January, dies, and is cremated at Golder's Green.

CHAPTER 1

Terra Incognita

I Early Life and Career

THE reader who enters Charles Montagu Doughty's world explores a terrain as mysterious and unknown as the Norwegian glaciers and nineteenth-century Arabian deserts which Doughty himself, with high courage, confronted. The traveler gleans easy knowledge of the immediate landscape but finds it difficult or impossible to penetrate to the interior. The facts of Doughty's life are known, but not the inner man. Because he destroyed the manuscript of *Travels in Arabia Deserta*, had few if any friends to write memoirs, and has left us only nearly illegible notebooks and some not very revealing letters, we plunge into his mind with few signposts to guide us. We do not know when he began to develop the unique stylistic ideology and intense interest in the past that led to his lifelong triple quest for the origins of man, nature, and himself. We do not know exactly why he went into Arabia determined to identify himself as a Christian in the face of a hostile population, or the exact processes by which he composed the final version of this story. We do not know why his many internal contradictions began and how they developed. And we have only one biography, D. G. Hogarth's posthumous *Life of Charles M. Doughty*,[1] which, however excellent, concentrates on the externals of its subject's life, as a guide. The search for Doughty the man parallels his own for the Arabia of his imagination which he frequently failed to find in the land bearing that name, and half a century after his death remains equally fascinating and frustrating.

The facts of Doughty's life and career help partially toward an understanding of the inner man, who is as reticent and elusive as his idealized personae, Khalil, the solitary "Friend of God" of *Arabia Deserta*, and Minimus, least important of men, of *Mansoul*, indicate. The circumstances of Doughty's childhood help explain his closed, solitary nature to some degree, for his mother died a few months after his

15

birth on 19 August 1843, and his clergyman father six years later, leaving Charles and his brother orphans—if well-provided ones—in the care of an uncle. Charles wanted to follow the tradition of his mother's religious and patriotic family and go to sea, was sent to the appropriate preparatory schools, but failed the navy medical examination in 1856 owing to a slight speech impairment. His ability to withstand solitude, adventurousness, capacity to bear physical hardship, and concern with the oral aspects of literature, most probably owe something to these facts.

In 1861 Doughty entered Gonville and Caius College, Cambridge, to study geology. A memoir by a fellow undergraduate describes him as "shy, nervous and very polite. He had no sense of humour, and I cannot remember that he had any literary tastes or leanings whatsoever."[2] We see these same qualities remaining constant throughout his life, with the exception of a biting irony that makes itself felt in *Arabia Deserta* and a very strong literary leaning that transformed him into a writer. In 1863, Doughty shifted to Downing College, Cambridge, where attendance at lectures and chapel was not required. He went to Norway at the end of the year to research glaciation, an experience that he recalls in *Arabia Deserta* for similarity of landscape. This journey resulted in a report to the British Association in 1864 and publication of his pamphlet "On the Jöstedal-brae Glaciers in Norway" in 1866. Despite Hogarth's praise of the style of this pamphlet, the reader will find very little in it to prepare him for the later magnificence of *Arabia Deserta;* and just when and how Doughty developed his unique prose cannot be pinpointed. In 1865 he took a "second" in the Tripos or final honors examination, failing to receive a "first" because of an inability or refusal to select rather than include details, a characteristic which operates in all his literary works. He returned to Caius and took his degree in 1866, apparently pleased to conclude studies which did not satisfy deeper but vague aspirations.

At some point in 1865 he had decided to write a patriotic work about Roman, Celtic, and German origins, and immediately upon graduation devoted himself to preparation for this task. He first studied independently in London and in 1868–1870 was reading older English literature and Erasmus in the Bodleian Library, Oxford, leading an ascetic and aloof life which was affected only externally by the depreciation of his family's investments and his subsequent near-penury. We see in the personality of Doughty at the age of twenty-seven the traits that would make it possible for him to travel with little money and alone (except for guides) through unknown parts of Arabia while declaring himself a Christian and even anti-Islam: a bare, serious, highly aspiring nature informed by an intense patriotism, love of the past, adventuresomeness, and devout but informal belief in God.

As we learn from the manuscript diary now in the possession of the Gonville and Caius Library, he spent 1871–1873 traveling as a studious "world-wanderer" (as he calls himself in *Arabia Deserta*) through Europe and North Africa. The diary records his presence at the eruption of Vesuvius in 1872, an event recorded retrospectively with great power in *Arabia Deserta*. He especially loved Italy and the Mediterranean world, frequently returning to live there in later life. He read the *Odyssey* in Massero's Italian translation and the many annotations in his copy (now in the Gonville and Caius Library) show his addiction to this ancient Mediterranean narrative of fantastic voyages.

From Italy, he headed for Spain via Sicily and North Africa, where he experienced his first encounter with the Arabs. Like the pamphlet on the Jöstedal-brae glacier, the diary gives us no reason to suspect that its author would develop into a great master of prose. But as Mrs. Ruth Robbins, the lifelong Doughty researcher, informed me,[3] certain passages of it provide a sign of nascent interest in Semitic things that may have contributed to his later decision to enter the Near East. In the summer of 1873 Doughty went to Italy again and then to Greece. We see him in all these travels displaying a restlessness and overcoming a weak physique which had prompted his father to have him immediately baptized upon birth; but no clear goal makes itself felt.

In Greece in 1874, he suddenly decided to plunge into the Levant. Unconsciously, he was in search of himself, which he could find only through the human and physical opposition of another culture and its land; but this is only one of many vague if more conscious motives. Perhaps, as Barker Fairley has suggested, he was already interested in getting to the deepest, pre-European core of civilization; perhaps his North African experience and discovered delight in Hellenism in Greece prompted him to try Hebraism, with a remembrance of the Bible from his childhood and more recent reading in the background; or possibly, as Hogarth suggests, he simply balked at the idea of returning to a damp England to face "life." Significantly for the Hebraism-Bible theory, he traveled first to Acre in what is now Israel, after having touched at the usual Turkish and Lebanese ports on the way, and went immediately to the classic sites of the Holy Land. Thus, he visited Carmel, Nazareth, Samaria, and Nablus on a journey to Jerusalem, and then headed for Bethlehem and Hebron before turning northward into the Galilee, Banias, and Damascus, finally returning to Jerusalem by way of Baalbek and Jaffa.

In autumn 1874 he left the Holy Land via El Arish and spent some time in Egypt before taking a three-month camel journey through the Sinai peninsula in 1875, a sojourn remembered in a brief report to the Royal Geographical Society of Austria,[4] in *Arabia Deserta* retrospectively, and, nearly half a century later, in *Mansoul*, where he stresses its harshness. Leaving Sinai in the northeast, he arrived at Maan and Nabataean Petra in what is now Jordan in May 1875. Here he heard of the inscriptions of Medain Salih and nearby Hejr, and resolved to return at a later date to make pressings of them, as he tells us in the opening section of *Arabia Deserta*.

II   *Travels in Arabia Deserta*

Arrived at Damascus, he found that no British organization was willing to sponsor his proposed trip to Medain Salih, and decided to study Arabic for a year and familiarize himself with a new culture. Despite the refusal of the British Royal Geographical Society and the British Association to provide him with funds, and a lack of help from the British and Turkish authorities in Damascus, he chose to make the trip anyway, with the added goal of studying Beduin life. On 10 November 1876 one of the most fantastic adventures ever recorded began when Khalil, as Doughty called himself in Arabia and in *Arabia Deserta*, "clothed as a Syrian of simple fortune"[5] and equipped with a few medicines to sell, left Damascus to join the pilgrim caravan southward. It was to end a long twenty-one months later, on 2 August 1878, when a Khalil much the worse for wear and persecution but unbowed spiritually emerged from the desert at the seaport of Jidda, far to the south.

Travels in Arabia Deserta records in twelve hundred pages of painstaking detail the course of Khalil's travels—which forms the basic plot of the book—beginning with the refusal of the British and Turkish officials to help him on his way, and the preparation and departure of the *Hâj*, or pilgrimage caravan, followed by Khalil's start two days later. The forty chapters contained in the two volumes of the book comprise nine plot sections. In the first of these (Volume 1, chapters 1–3), Khalil joins the caravan and learns its customs and fables, as well as the topography of Edom and Arabia Petraea through which it passes on its way to Medain Salih and the Holy Cities. The narrator dwells on the biblical account of the clash between Hebrews and Edomites, the geology of the land, Khalil's difficulties as a Christian among the "hajjies," or pilgrims, and the interest of the new sights, sounds, customs, and tales that confronted Khalil. Despite some perhaps retrospective pique on the part of the narrator, the tone of writing is light.

Chapters 4–7 describe Khalil's experience of life in the *kella*, or caravan way station, at Medain Salih, including his relationship with its inhabitants, particularly old Haj Nejm the gatekeeper and the towerkeeper Mohammed Aly, and his half-exciting, half-disappointing exploration of the Medain Salih Nabataean monuments. The narrator emphasizes Khalil's difficulty in distinguishing between reality and miragelike illusion during this first real taste of life on the edge of Arabia. An ostensibly rational Mohammed Aly explodes into violence, which Khalil controls through his personal method of passive resistance. A visit to the nearby town of El Ally is described in unusually full detail because this is Khalil's first encounter with an Arabian township.

Chapters 8–13 of volume 1 relate Khalil's stay with Sheikh Zeyd of the Fejir or Fukara Beduins. Khalil at the end of chapter 7 has sent his completed "squeezing" of the monuments back to Damascus with the returning caravan, but refuses to accompany it despite everyone's warnings and urgings. With Zeyd, Khalil learns all the details of nomadic survival and domestic customs, even playing go-between to retrieve Zeyd's disaffected wife, Hirfa, when she leaves her husband. Despite some differences with Zeyd over a camel and the generally straitened circumstances of life with a Beduin tribe, we feel in the comic incidents and occasional humor and freedom of feeling in these chapters Khalil's pleasure in Beduin ways, and he manages to extend his knowledge of inner Arabia by visiting Teyma with the Beduin.

His original goals fulfilled, Khalil is ready to leave Arabia by the first week of May 1877. But he must wait three weeks in the *kella* where Zeyd leaves him until arrangements can be made to forward him to the seaport of Wejh. Hearing of a caravan of Fukara Beduins going there, he leaves to join them, but illness intervenes and he finds himself too sick to travel the hundred miles to Wejh. As a result, he stays with the Moahib Beduins, who are camped on the Harra, or lava field, near Medain Salih. Without knowing it, he finds himself committed to another full year's stay in Arabia.

The four summer months that Khalil spent with the Moahib and then some Fukara and Welad Aly Beduins and his trip to Hayil,

Mohammed Ibn Rashid's capital, fill chapters 14–21 of volume 1. Despite some trouble in securing Sheikh Tollog's approval to remain with his tribe, he manages to stay with them. He enjoys this life so much that he abandons the idea of leaving Arabia. Instead he broods over the attainment of the city of Kheybar, focal point of legends about ancient Jews, which had been on his mind since his original stay at the *kella*. This section includes troubles with Horeysh, one of a series of treacherous guides, and Khalil's suffering caused by near-famine conditions among the Moahib. After a time with the Fukara and Welad Aly, he manages to leave for Teyma (where he experienced relatively good treatment from the people, but also a frightening spell of near-blindness) and (in chapter 21) arrives in Hayil and has his first audience with the great ruler of northern Arabia, Mohammed Ibn Rashid.

The last part of chapter 21 and all of chapter 22 of the first volume, and chapters 1, 2, and the first part of 3 of the second, detail Khalil the *Nasrâny's* (or Christian) experience of court life in north Arabia. He becomes more familiar with Mohammed Ibn Rashid and his relative and adviser Hamud, who show great intelligence and prescience in pressing Khalil about the possible value of petroleum and the precise workings of Western technological wonders like electricity. In his role as wandering *hakîm,* or physician, he cures Hamud's child. He learns the history of the family, which has only recently included a series of assassinations culminating in Mohammed's rise to the throne. The narrator portrays this story as a high tragedy in which Mohammed Ibn Rashid plays the role of the good and intelligent man forced to perform bloody deeds which may in turn doom him, and Khalil later calls Mohammed "'a worthy man.'" But Khalil's open European pride and stubborn failure to show obeisance to the Emir Mohammed, combined perhaps with the ruler's perspicacious suspicion of British colonialism and the restiveness of a hostile and ignorant population, result in the Christian's sudden expulsion from the town. Here as elsewhere he has resisted the entreaty to become or at least appear to become a Moslem, with a doggedness bordering on masochism. At the time of his expulsion from Hayil (20 November 1877), he has been in Arabia for one full year.

Finally arrived at Kheybar after urging his unsteady guide, Ghroceyb, onward, Khalil finds the atmosphere of this legendary city poisonous in every way. Chapters 3–8 of volume 2 are devoted to Khalil's travails in this one town. Instead of the fantastic city of fabulous legend, he comes to a poor village infested with a chronic fever caused by a poor water supply and terrorized by a corrupt Turkish commandant, Abdullah. Abdullah, with the aid of his brutal servant Sirur, keeps Khalil a virtual prisoner from the end of November until the middle of March, while the question of his life or death hangs on the decision of the Pasha of Medina. The lone friendship of Mohammed en Nejumy makes his life in Kheybar more bearable, but he experiences little outside of fear and insult until the enlightened Pasha despatches a letter commanding that he be freed and sent back to Hayil.

The Gothic tones and details of the narration of this whole episode, including a series of very fine djinn tales, brilliantly convey the atmosphere besetting Khalil. In Kheybar as elsewhere high expectations of Arabia are brutally disappointed by reality. However, simple escape alone is never on Khalil's mind. Even now, he wants to go to Bahrein and thence to India, thus accomplishing the West-East crossing of Arabia even on his way out.

Although he basks in Beduin freedom after having left Kheybar, he has more trouble with the guides appointed to take him back to Hayil; and when he arrives there this second time, Aneybar, the chamberlain of Mohammed Ibn Rashid, refuses to forward him to Bahrein and instead sends him back to Kheybar! Chapters 9–11 of the second volume recount this return to Hayil, expulsion, trouble with guides who desert him, and arrival in Boreyda instead of Kheybar. Here he is attacked by a savage populace from which he barely escapes, and departs the next morning for Aneyza.

As Khalil penetrates deeper into Arabia, his troubles increase; and this growing tension, felt in the second volume, provides a good deal of the suspense and interest of the whole tale. Chapters 12–16 set forth Khalil's fate in the important town of Aneyza where he arrives after leaving Boreyda, its traditional rival. At first, relief appears. Zamil, the town's ruler, receives him well, and he quickly builds a clientele for his medical practice. Even better, he makes friends with Abdullah el Kenneyny and Abdullah el Bessam, wealthy and aware merchants, and their younger friends of the upper class. He enjoys talks about politics and culture in an amenable atmosphere. But with the incitement of the town's preachers, the people slowly turn against him. He is driven out, recalled, and finally departs with a merchant caravan for Mecca and the coast. The biting tone of the narration of these haps—worthy of a satirical Dutch master painter—and the milder irony surrounding other incidents in this section underline Khalil's growing exhaustion and tension.

Near Mecca—which he as a Christian is forbidden to enter—at the end of chapter 16, Khalil is threatened by Sheikh Salem and his cohort Fheyd in his most frightening adventure. Chapters 16–18 of volume 2 thus contain the climactic action of the whole book. Under the guise of religious duty, Salem continually menaces Khalil with a knife and finally with Khalil's own pistol in the hope of stealing Khalil's camel and goods. But Khalil's appearance of nonchalance and Christian forebearance—augmented by the support of Maabub, servant of the Sherif of Mecca—win him his life until he arrives, sick and weary, at Tayif for a judgment by the Sherif. In a classic case of justice done, the Sherif punishes Salem and Fheyd and rewards Khalil with offers of aid in further travel. Amazingly, Khalil is mentally more than ready to go on to the Wadi Duwasir and even the dangerous Rub al Khali or Empty Quarter (which was not crossed until Bertram Thomas did it in 1931), but must decline because he is simply too sick to go on. Khalil's final descent in Arab dress to the port of Jidda and his invitation by the British officialdom which had rejected him at the outset of his journey, thus causing a good part of his troubles, concludes *Travels in Arabia Deserta* abruptly and ironically.

The reader has witnessed in amazing detail one of the great triumphs of the spirit of all time, even if the motivation for it and especially for Khalil's refusal to mask the fact that he was a Christian, thus making life doubly hard for himself, remain shrouded in mystery. The narrator never lets us in on the inner workings of Khalil's mind, or his own. Seen simplistically in modern psychological terms—a treatment which Doughty, an Englishman of the old Victorian heroic school, has so far escaped, perhaps luckily—Doughty in *Arabia Deserta* appears to display an inherent masochistic streak, reinforced by his identification with puritanical Christian models. We can also say that his determination to prove that he could survive all the suffering an impossibly harsh human and physical climate could mete out was a proof to himself that he was worthy of the naval career which he longed for until the end of his life and never attained. And that only by means of such a test could he determine and develop his own personality and beliefs.

Doughty's sense of irony at his reception by the British consul in Jidda was scarcely lessened by his treatment in England, where he arrived after a stay in an Indian hospital spent recovering from the exhaustion, opthalmia, and bilharzia he had contracted in Arabia. While in Bombay, he had read to the Royal Asiatic Society branch there a paper on his journey (published in its journal for 1878), but the Royal Geographical Society in England did not receive him particularly well. Nor was it interested in his Nabataean inscriptions. So his first articles on his explorations appeared in the German periodical *Globus* in 1880–1882,[6] and his Nabataean work came out as *Documents épigraphiques recueillis dans le nord de l'Arabie* (1884) under the auspices of the scholar Ernest Renan and the Paris Académie des Inscriptions. He did not even address the Royal Geographical Society until 1883, and received its award only in 1912! And *Arabia Deserta*, upon which he worked from 1879 until its publication in 1888, scarcely got better treatment: rejected by four commercial publishers because of its style, it was accepted only after much discussion by Cambridge University Press, which failed to sell very many copies.

The book's first reviewers realized that they were dealing with something unique and important, but could not come to terms with its unusual style, as the anonymous critic of the *Westminster Review* reveals:

The narrative of his intercourse with the wild dwellers in these seldom-visited regions is so minute, Mr. Doughty's mind is so thoroughly saturated with Arab thought and speech and habit, that we may safely say no Englishman has given us such an insight into these as Mr. Doughty has done. But for some reason, which we cannot explain, he writes in a style and tongue peculiar to himself—a picturesque quasi-scriptural style—which has its charm indeed when one is accustomed to it, but which, coupled with a very free use of Arabic words, somewhat enhances the general reader's difficulty in following the curious narrative of exploration and adventure which fills these two large volumes.[7]

Arabia Deserta lapsed immediately into obscurity—outside of the appreciation of the few like Wilfrid Blunt, William Morris, Edward Burne-Jones, and Robert Bridges who were engaged in similar artistic experiments—until Edward Garnett's 330,000 word abridgment, *Wanderings in the Desert*, revived it in 1908.

From the publication of *Arabia Deserta* until his death, Doughty wrote only one more piece of prose, a review of D. G. Hogarth's book *Arabia*, which testifies that he remained at the end of his life as deep an antiquarian as ever, calling "the days" of "Abraham . . ." not "very remote."[8] His life after his return from Arabia was uneventful and devoted to poetry, regarded by Doughty as his major vocation—fortunately or unfortunately depending upon the critic's evaluation of his respective prosaic and poetic abilities.

III   *Later Life and Poetic Career*

In 1900, his slim volume of hackneyed, chauvinistic verse, *Under Arms 1900,* privately printed through the Army and Navy Stores, and intended to buttress patriotic zeal for the Boer War, appeared. Even Doughty's most ardent poetic partisans prefer to exclude this volume from their purview because of its low quality of thought and versification. While writing and publishing this small book and earlier, Doughty was preoccupied with a much larger but similarly patriotic project, the composition of an epic of early Britain, which had been on his mind since college days, as we have seen. Finally in 1906–1907 *The Dawn in Britain* appeared, largely through the good offices of Edward Garnett, then a reader for Duckworth and Co. Despite a largely enthusiastic reception of its deliberately rough, neo-primitive style and mythological-heroic content, we detect a mixed note on the part of some reviewers, which was to prove prophetic. In a comment to be echoed by many subsequent critics, R. C. Lehmann in the *Bookman* found that "Here and there, like gleams of sunshine from a stormy sky, there are passages of real poetry, but they are few, and to search for them is difficult."[9] Whatever the attitude of early reviewers, the poem has lapsed into total oblivion outside of a University of Toronto cult audience and other isolated enthusiasts.

This poem of 30,000 ten-syllable lines was followed in 1908 by *Adam Cast Forth,* a "sacred drama," which is based on a Moslem legend about Adam and Eve and has the advantage of being much more direct and unstereotyped than *Dawn in Britain.* Here Doughty presses his search for the past back beyond even the origins of British civilization and Beduin patriarchs to man's earliest ancestors. However much Doughty the Victorian continued to look down on Arabia with assumed cultural superiority, the East brought out the best in him artistically, and the desert suffering recaptured in the drama strikes a note of absolute authenticity lacking in his other poetry. Initially well received, it has retained the admiration of subsequent critics who, like Middleton Murry, found little to admire in the rest of Doughty's poetic output, but it has suffered the same fate of general neglect as all the other poems.

Always interested in technological innovation, like any man of his age, and a fervent British patriot as we have seen, Doughty kept a careful eye on European science and politics which belies the totally antiquarian image sometimes projected by commentators on his personality. If *Arabia Deserta, Dawn in Britain,* and *Adam Cast Forth* can be seen as journeys into the past, the next two poetic dramas, *The Cliffs* (1909) and *The Clouds* (1912) represent an early form of science fiction, in which Doughty as poetic *vates* or seer correctly predicted World War I and its use of the submarine, mine, airship, torpedo, and other technical developments with great accuracy, even looking forward to our period of lasers. Although they were received well during (but not before) the war for their novelty value, we now see the poetic quality of these works as extremely low, owing to their patriotic excess (child sacrifice in *The Cliffs,* glory or death in *The Cliffs* and *The Clouds*), stilted archaic dialogue forced to express contemporary action, and coincidental and vague structure. The poems remain an interesting excursion into popular art, rather on the level of sentimental and bloody comic books, and show that Doughty could react to an imagined attack on Britain with no less fanaticism than he attributes to the Arabs in *Arabia Deserta.*

The Titans (1916) unsuccessfully mixes the antiquarian and science fiction veins in a muddy way as Doughty brings us back beyond even Adam and Eve to the very formation of the earth, when giants stalk the land and battle finally and unvictoriously with the sons of men for control. *Mansoul* (1920; revised 1923) remained Doughty's own favorite among his works, and amounts to a medieval dream vision in which the poet as the persona Minimus describes a clichéd but sometimes beautifully gentle journey into the underworld marred by low-level philosophical speculation and outbursts against the kaiser.

In his entire corpus, taken as a whole, we see the contradictions of the man himself: antiquarianism but belief in technological "progress"; masochistic self-effacement in Arabia but sadistically bloody battles and beliefs in *Dawn in Britain, The Cliffs, The Clouds,* and even *Mansoul;* science versus religion; desired love of humanity and yet a very intolerant patriotism and religion. These varying qualities exist side by side in separate compartments deep below the surface of his mind and appear only in the art. Visitors to his household speak only of the calm outer life enjoyed by Doughty, who had married happily in 1886 and had two daughters, and his patriarchal demeanor and benevolent smiles. Although recognition finally came to him in the form of the Gold Medal of the Royal Geographical Society (1912), honorary degrees from both Oxford (1908) and Cambridge (1920), membership in the British Academy (1922), and the warm admiration of some younger contemporaries like the youthful (but not older) T. E. Lawrence, he remained necessitous almost to the end of his life, when he received an inheritance. He was forced to move about frequently, as the suitcase in the Gonville and Caius Library, used to hold the "General Word Notes" he compiled, sadly testifies.

We may see in the man both the best and the worst of the old imperial England, which was fast declining at the time of his death on 20 January 1926—great courage, belief, honesty, self-reliance, and technological superiority; but also class and cultural arrogance and closed-mindedness. Doughty remained, at least on the conscious level, a conservative Victorian who lived into the twentieth century without modifying his views. He provides proof that knowledge of technology does not necessarily lead to spiritual progress or tolerance, but also that a radical conservatism can be just as artistically fruitful as avant-gardism. In *Arabia Deserta*, his one indisputably great work, we read his own gnarled, massive, faulted personality as much as we read Arabia, and feel, as in Walt Whitman's case, that one who touches this work "touches a man," and that we will not see so cranky—and great—an individualist soon again.

CHAPTER 2

Travels in Arabia Deserta:
Literary Landscape

A radical conservatism in art as in life can prove just as "revolutionary" as the most ambitious leftism. Charles Doughty believed that the language and literature of England had come to a period of decline and fall after the time of Edmund Spenser and the King James Bible, but produced in *Arabia Deserta* a book as contemporary, original, and profound as that of any writer of his period, the fin de siècle. Far more than an exotic curiosity of literature, *Arabia Deserta* displays the same complex links to a tradition and to its own period that we find in any great work. And it is no more a "curiosity" in its striking uniqueness than any masterpiece of prose. A knowledge of the forces acting on Doughty the artist, his method of composing, the precise nature of his final achievement and its relationship to other late Victorian works of art reveals its genuine originality and spares us a view of *Arabia Deserta* as a merely exotic and inexplicable excrescence on the English literary tradition.

I *Influences and Similarities*

When Khalil must "cast away the superfluous weight" (II, 279) of his books in an attempt to leave Arabia, he retains only Alois Sprenger's *Die Alte Geographie Arabiens* of 1875 (which he terms, after his beloved Erasmus, "my enchiridion in these travels," I, 54), a scholarly account of the map of ancient Arabia; Albrecht Zehme's *Arabien und die Araber Seit Hundert Jahren* (1875), a secondary history of recent European exploration of Arabia; a standard 1876 Eyre & Spottiswoode edition of the King James Bible; and "several leaves" from Chaucer's *Canterbury Tales,* in Speght's 1687 black-letter edition.[1] In their representation of scientific, religious, and literary interests, these books reveal the three major kinds of influence operating on Doughty throughout his life.

A   Scientific Influences

As the many passages of *Arabia Deserta* devoted to precise geography, geology, and a kind of primitive unrelativistic cultural and physical anthropology testify, Doughty's most apparent (but not most important) reason for Arabian travels was scientific. He wished to solve geographical and archeological problems posed by ancient and modern mapmakers and explorers—like the true direction of Arabian watercourses and the precise locations of ancient cities—and which are expounded in the pages of Zehme's history and the thin and handy but densely packed work by Sprenger, which comprises 314 pages of numbered paragraphs and concludes with a copy of Ptolemy's map of Arabia.[2] Although Doughty's copy of Sprenger's work has unfortunately been lost, we can tell from the six references to it in *Arabia Deserta* that Doughty used it to learn the ancient origins of modern cities that he saw, as well as the ancient customs of the area. This interest in ancient history reveals that under Doughty's modern geographical quest lies an intense antiquarian obsession with the origin of civilizations.

But Doughty's quest for the past does not stop with civilizations. As Richard Bevis has pointed out in an article on Doughty's scientific background, Doughty is really concerned with Arabian exploration, because it is in Arabia's bare topography that one "was closer to, because more aware of, the Creator" in Bevis's words. Under the personalized influence of Charles Lyell, author of the *Principles of Geology* (1830) which Doughty studied at Cambridge, and, more vaguely, Charles Darwin, Doughty, according to Bevis, comes to see geology and natural selection as signs of God's actual presence in the world. Nature for Doughty becomes, as Bevis puts it, a "Scourge of God. It turns on man a face of awful and seldom-relenting hostility, but from this clash is born a rapport with the divine, so that the encounter is religious and ultimately beneficial for man."[3] In Arabia man sees God at work on the face of the land most directly and confronts him most nakedly in Doughty's vision. Further, the all-pervasive importance of the Bible for him, which we shall soon discuss, dictates Arabia and the Arabic language as the closest approach to God possible in his time.

Sprenger's book informed Doughty of human history in Arabia, and

Lyell and Darwin, in his use of them, of divine history being written into the skeleton of the land and its creatures. But Doughty needed immediate practical knowledge of previous explorations of Arabia, and for this he turned to Zehme's 400-page survey of major Arabian explorations of the hundred years preceding its publication in 1875.[4] Zehme gives a compressed synopsis and evaluation of the scientific contribution of each traveler, so that W. G. Palgrave, for instance, who took over nine hundred pages to recount his own adventures, receives a bare thirty-five pages which concentrate solely on his geography. The fact that Doughty was satisfied to use Zehme's secondary history rather than consult the works of his predecessors directly indicates that he was interested only in their scientific contributions. Unlike T. E. Lawrence, who literally learned to write about the desert from such works as Palgrave's *Narrative* of his travels and *Arabia Deserta* itself, and whose interest in travel books was at least as literary as it was scientific, Doughty felt that he had nothing literary to learn from accounts written in what was for him decadent nineteenth-century language. So, with the exception of J. L. Burckhardt's work, which he appears to have read, he was content with Zehme's relatively brief summaries of the journeys of his predecessors.

Although his personal copy of Zehme's work—like his Sprenger— has been lost or misplaced, we can guess the degree of his reliance upon it from the comment he makes in the first preface of *Arabia Deserta* itself. There he writes that the accounts of Wallin, Palgrave, and Guarmani were "when I sojourned in Arabia (and since) . . . known to me only in A. Zehme's excellent treatise." While the Swede George Augustus Wallin's two dry reports to the Royal Geographical Society and the Italian work of Carlo Guarmani could hold little literary interest for an English travel writer, William Gifford Palgrave's (1826–1888) sensational and best-selling *Narrative of a Year's Journey through Central and Eastern Arabia* (1862–1863) displays a fine style and flamboyant use of the personality, combined with truly fantastic and daring explorations and escapes, which mark it as a work of art from which any writer would have something to learn.[5] As a thrilling and well-written record of adventures and autobiography it ranks with Kinglake's *Eothen*, Doughty's *Arabia Deserta*, Lawrence's *Seven Pillars of Wisdom*, and Thesiger's *Arabian Sands* as one of the "big five" artistic Anglo-Arabian travel works.[6] At most, however, Palgrave exerted only a marginal scientific influence and a negative literary influence on Doughty, as we learn from the latter's letter of 18 January

1892 to Guy Le Strange: "I have read the compendium in Zehme but
not his [Palgrave's] work except that part which deals with er-Riath;
but I think he describes the Nejd town-dwellers to the life. I could
make nothing of his map and was repelled from his volumes by his air
of *habile homme*."[7]

If he had nothing of style, self-characterization, or map-making to
learn from Palgrave in his opinion, Doughty might have been able to
absorb tolerance and cultural relativity from the remarkable *Travels
through Arabia* (1792) of the great Danish-German scientist and
explorer Carsten Niebuhr (died 1815), one of the few travelers to
understand the purist Islamic movement, Wahabism, which began in
the eighteenth century, sympathetically. But we find no references to
Doughty's having actually read or been impressed by Niebuhr's work,
possibly because it is concerned with Yemen and the Tehama region
only, and Doughty traveled mainly in northern Arabia.

Similarly, Doughty ignored the work of Sir Richard Francis Burton
(1821–1890), the semi-Moslem convert and able Arabist (who knew
fifty-seven other languages!), as Burton himself tells us in a scathing
review of Doughty's book: "Mr. Doughty informed me that he has not
read what I have written upon Arabia; and that I regret more for his
sake than for my own. My 'Pilgrimage' would have saved him many
an inaccuracy. . . ."[8] While Burton's *Personal Narrative of a Pilgrimage to Al Madinah and Mecca* (1855–1856) falls short of the greatest
Anglo-Arabian works both artistically and scientifically, his brilliant
linguistic ability far exceeded Doughty's and might well have been
useful to the later traveler. But, thinking Burton's prose would be of no
interest to him, Doughty read only Zehme's sparse account of Burton's
work.

Doughty as writer was cavalier in his disregard of most of his
immediate predecessors' own tales of their explorations. But he did
well in ignoring totally the popular tradition of literary "Orientalism"
already well established by his time. As Martha Conant's *The Oriental
Tale in England in the Eighteenth Century*[9] makes clear, Antoine
Galland's French translation of the *Arabian Nights* made a very deep
impression on the eighteenth century and the romantic movement all
over Europe. The "Oriental" atmosphere of Johnson's *Rasselas* and
Beckford's Gothic novel *Vathek*, as well as poems like Thomas Moore's
"Lalla Rookh," Southey's "Thalaba the Destroyer," and many works
of Byron, present a popularized and false image of the Near East that
Doughty dismisses with several biting comments in *Arabia Deserta*, as

when he writes that "in Arabia . . . is so little (or nothing) of *Oriental-ism*" (I, 579).

But a certain subconscious influence common to both the scientific and the popular European-Arabian literature did seep into Doughty's mind, possibly through Zehme and the one previous traveler whom he definitely appears to have read and whom he names "the worthy Burckhardt" (I, 40) and cites, alone among travelers, twice in *Arabia Deserta*. Johann Ludwig Burckhardt (died 1817), gifted and energetic Swiss scientist and linguist, became the first European to attain the red Nabataean city of Petra and remains one of the few who meticulously and accurately described Jidda, Taif, Mecca, and Medina as prepara-tion for his never-achieved goal of exploring African geography in depth for the British Africa Association. Like Doughty himself, Burck-hardt carried on in the face of physical infirmity, and died after a two-year illness caused by his travels, a fate Doughty only barely escaped. Since like Palgrave and Burton, Burckhardt disguised himself as an Arab, he suffered less from a hostile population than did Doughty, who masochistically insisted on his role as *Nasrâny;* but climate and disease alone were enough to debilitate him. He left behind only his posthu-mous *Travels in Arabia* (1829) and *Notes on the Bedouins and Wahabys* (1831), books notable for their total suppression of his per-sonality, lack of adventure, and unerring accuracy; they are memoirs, or external histories of his travels, rather than artistic travel autobiography.[10]

However realistic and accurate Burckhardt is, his books reinforce two images of the Arabs which must be termed "romantic" rather than objective: that of the "racial" purity and aristocracy of the Bedouin and town sheikhs on the one hand and the use of the word "fanatic" to characterize Islam, particularly that of the Wahabi variety, on the other. We see the positive image of the Arab ruler when Burckhardt writes that the Sherifs of Mecca are "distinguished by fine manly coun-tenances, strongly expressive of noble extraction. . . ."[11] Palgrave too, for instance, found the Arabs generally "one of the noblest races the earth affords" and a similar approving pseudo-scientific class vision lies behind Doughty's characterization of Beduin sheikhs in particular: "The sheukh . . . are nobles of the blood . . ." (I, 251). The unqualified phrase "nobles of the blood" reveals Doughty's own belief in aristoc-racy under an ostensibly objective description.

Despite the reservations of all these travelers regarding incidents of Beduin and town dwellers' rapacity and treachery, they pass on to the reader a view of the desert in which the noble image is very prominent. In fact, European visions of the nobility and blue blood of desert sheikhs and town rulers testify primarily to a European desire to see the declining nineteenth-century class system, pseudo-genetic theories of aristocratic "blood" and "race," and the romantic "noble savage" doctrine affirmed, and provide strong evidence of lingering memories of the Richard Coeur-de-Lion and Saladin stories of the Crusades. It might be possible to see in the Beduins even today the tough and hardy warriorlike qualities that T. E. Lawrence in particular praises. But just as we would be hard-pressed to demonstrate that blue blood ran in the veins of European aristocracy, so we would have trouble finding it in desert sheikhs' arteries. No matter how factually accurate and realistically intended, European accounts of the desert, especially in the nineteenth century, inevitably include an ideologically colored and consequently heightened vision.

The other side of this coin we see in Burckhardt's utterance " . . . the domes were invariably broken down by the Wahabys; these fanatics, however . . . ,"[12] and Doughty's persistent strictures against "a fanatical religion" (xii). As Anne Treneer has noted, the word "fanatic" becomes a key word of Doughty's whole book. While no one can deny that the stricter sects of Islam are frequently intolerant and narrow— in the manner of Calvinism, which Burton compared them to—or that Doughty and other travelers suffered much from their hosts' religious ignorance, prejudice, and provincialism, the use of the magic word "fanatic" conjures up a totally irrational "mysterious East" in Western minds. Like any stereotypical term, it has no place in a truly scientific-anthropological vocabulary. Only Niebuhr, as Hogarth has pointed out in his *Penetration of Arabia* (1904), attained a just understanding of the Wahabies instead of substituting a mythical Western image of "fanaticism" for Arabian reality, although it must be added that when he traveled Islamic xenophobia was at a minimum.

In this twin stereotype of Arabian nobility and fanaticism we see the elements of literary romance and epic Crusader memories and nineteenth-century ideology entering the accounts of even honest Western observers without their being aware of it. Thus, Doughty's reading of the relatively mild and unpoetic Burckhardt, like his religiously based geographical science, led him toward a nonobjective, antiquarian, literary view of the Arabs and their land even as his aneroid readings and description of Arabian watercourses are professionally perfect for their time. Despite Doughty's scrupulously honest attempt to be accurate, T. E. Lawrence's comment that "Doughty's book mirrored Doughty as much as it mirrored Arabia"[13] is true in more ways than one.

B Religious Influences

D. G. Hogarth writes that "Doughty, as his letters show, was an agnostic Humanitarian of heart-felt piety and deep reverence for any credo based on Reason."[14] Despite Hogarth's use of letters, the objective observer may feel that he has read a view of Khalil's occasionally professed universalism and agnosticism into the man who wrote *Arabia Deserta*. In fact, a careful look at both *Arabia Deserta's* hero Khalil and its narrator and the collection of Doughty's books in the Gonville and Caius College Library leads us to see devout belief in Christianity as a far more important influence on Doughty the man, artist, and protagonist than Hogarth reveals.

In *Arabia Deserta* itself, Khalil never denies—but rather affirms on several occasions—a belief in God. He is always prepared to attest to the idea that "God is one," but draws the line at calling Mohammed his prophet. This raises the interesting question of what would have happened had the blunt-talking Khalil been an open atheist or even Hogarth's "agnostic Humanitarian" rather than the certain believer in God who constantly appears before us: that would have been the *real* test of Khalil's ability to always speak truth. But he never has to face it because he has no trouble freely admitting his belief, and this firm belief alone makes him more than Hogarth's agnostic. However, Khalil is even more devout than a simple belief in God indicates. If we accept his statement to Ahmed in Kheybar, that Jesus' fathering remains "'a mystery which no tongue can unfold: which is to say he had none in our common understanding, except ye would say ULLAH'" (II, 159), Khalil also accepted the Virgin Birth as fact in spite of his oft-stated scientific impatience with (Moslem) "miracles." And then we have the evidence of Doughty's poetry, in which God is inevitably on Britain's side during wars, Joseph of Arimithea is mawkishly sentimentalized (in *Dawn in Britain*) for his Christian virtue and belief, Adam and Hawwa (in *Adam Cast Forth*) remain unhesitatingly obedient to the word of God, and a militant faith in science rather schizophrenically coexists (in *Mansoul*) with unquestioning religious belief without the slightest contact or conflict.

The 1876 King James Bible in the Gonville and Caius Doughty collection and the collection's more than ten Bibles in as many languages and assorted old Christian prayer books, reveal a biblical interest unusually deep even for a romantic nineteenth-century antiquarian. The number of biblical references in *Arabia Deserta's* style and content already testifies to Doughty's bedrock attachment to this ancient book, but we also have evidence in this collection (in the form of Doughty's Hebrew Bible and grammar book) that he diligently began learning Hebrew in 1906 at the age of sixty-three, in order to read the Old Testament in the original.[15] And we should also remember in assessing the depth of his belief that although he was orphaned early, his family background remained one of religion and patriotism.

The copy of the King James Bible that Doughty carried with him through Arabia reveals in the heavy annotations and underlinings in his handwriting the precise magnetism that it exerted on him as man and artist. We see clearly that he obsessively desires a "living experience"(as he puts it in *Arabia Deserta's* third preface) of biblical ways, that the New Testament rather than the Old—contrary to what Bevis states in his article—inspires Khalil's beliefs and mode of behavior in Arabia, and that the literary beauty of the Bible challenged Doughty the artist to attempt to write his own spiritual testament of moral quest in a style and vision rivaling its own. Although Doughty read the 1578 Geneva Bible and preferred its linguistic period, he chose this standard King James version (1611) to accompany him in the desert. Why? As Mrs. Robbins commented to me, the fact is that only this edition was readily available to him just before his departure from Syria, since thousands were shipped to the East as aids to missionary activity; and the King James was in any case a beloved familiar from his youth which would thus be particularly welcome during strange adventures.

The most obvious aspect of this Bible and the easiest to summarize remains Doughty's impulse toward Arabian exploration as a "living experience" of biblical customs, similar to Holman Hunt's desire to paint biblical scenes in the Holy Land itself. We find that the earliest layer of the Bible, the Pentateuch, is the most heavily marked, and with comments relating directly to customs witnessed by Khalil among the inhabitants of desert and town in Arabia. Thus, Exod. 1:16, about birth customs, has the word "stools" underlined and "as now in Syria" written next to it. The annotations "Arab midda" near Lev. 27:8 and "Hijab" near Num. 5:23,24 refer to equivalent practices—ransom money and medicinal amulets—mentioned in *Arabia Deserta* and the Bible.

We also notice everywhere in his Bible markings relating to the biblical lands themselves. Thus he notes the ores of rocks as he interprets biblical passages (underlining Deut. 9:9 and writing "stones are iron" in the margin), writes contemporary Arabic place-names next to the Hebrew ("Kabur" near the Hebrew "Kibroth" in Num. 11:34), and explains Old Testament poetic figures in a modern scientific manner (writing "the ground water . . . inside . . . earth" beside Deut. 33:13 and "? volcanoes in Arabia" next to Nah. 1:5).

He also indicates his own feeling for Beduin life and contemporary practices by underlining and annotating quotations of a more spiritual nature. He underlines the word "wealthy" in Jer. 49:31 and writes "!Beduw" in the margin next to this verse, which reads: "Arise, get you up unto the wealthy nation, that dwelleth without care, saith the Lord, which have neither gates nor bars, which dwell alone." This verse sums up Doughty's whole feeling about what Khalil calls in *Arabia Deserta* the best way of life in the world, poor outwardly but rich in freedom, and Doughty's exclamation mark indicates the thrill of realizing that his own feeling precisely matches the Bible's.

As much as Doughty warms to the thrill of antiquity, he condemns the cruelties of biblical kings and prophets alike. Thus, he marks Isa. 34:5–15 and Ezek. 35:3–10, 14, 15 (especially 3, 4, and most of all, 5), all of which relate God's curses against the Idumeans and Mt. Seir. In *Arabia Deserta* (I, 44), Doughty quotes in full the passages he underlined in his Bible in a kind of collage of curses and the narrator comments on them (I, 38) that "The Hebrew prophets at all times rail with bitter enmity of evil neighbourhood against the Peraean countries. . . ." He writes on I, 43 that "Edom and Jeshurun are rivals, and great was the cruelty of Hebrew arms in these countries." In his underlinings of Isa. 55:13 and 62:4 we see his humanitarian hope that waste lands would be renewed instead of further destroyed.

Doughty's aversion to what he considered Hebrew barbarism appears most clearly in his markings in 1 and 2 Sam. Near 1 Sam. 27:9, where David kills all living creatures among the Geshurites, Gezrites, and Amalekites, Doughty places an exclamation point. At 1 Sam. 30:2, where David shows mercy to the women of Ziklag, he writes "humanity" and an illegible word. At 2 Sam. 22:22, when David says "For I have kept the ways of the Lord, and have not wickedly departed from my God," Doughty's exclamation point clearly indicates ironic disbelief in either David's honesty, his conception of God, or both.

We infer from his biblical annotations—and the "Jesu" word-note

parcel which will be discussed under "Composition"—that Doughty
regards the Old Testament as largely a history of barbarism and the
God therein depicted as less spiritual than the God of the New Testament. We find few openly approving rather than neutral or negative
comments in the older document, and more approbation in Doughty's
New Testament. This typically biased view of Doughty's period, while
not an accurate perception of the Old Testament, affords us further
proof that Doughty was a man of his own time and the Christian
tradition.

Although most New Testament markings refer to objective comparison of Semitic customs then and now, Doughty sometimes goes
beyond these to indicate the depth of his attachment to Jesus and his
doctrines, and particularly to St. Paul's life and teachings. Near Luke
5:36, he writes "J. brought a new doctrine," an apparently neutral
comment referring to the obvious meaning of the parable in the passage. But in Luke 11:1 "teach us to pray" is underlined, and Doughty
writes "Not taught before!" thus stressing the attractive newness of
Jesus' message. Near the title of the Gospel according to St. John, he
writes "This gospel especially sets forth the divinity of Jeshua." The
use of the name "Jeshua" instead of Jesus perhaps indicates Doughty's
closeness to this idea, because Jeshua (Jesus' original Hebrew name) is
the name he uses constantly in his poetry for Jesus. John 6:38 has the
line "For I came down from heaven" (referring to Jesus) underlined,
with an exclamation point nearby. While we cannot state with cer-
tainty that these two last notations prove that Doughty believed in the
divinity of Jesus because there exists the possibility that the exclamation point at least is ironic, if we take these indications with all the
other evidence, they point at the minimum to a deep faith in Jesus
going beyond mere "agnostic Humanitarianism" into profound Christianity. Thus, we almost expect the large "X" at John 14:6: "Jesus saith
unto him, I am the way, the truth, and the life: no man cometh unto
the Father, but by me."

The St. Paul theme forms an important part of *Arabia Deserta*, as
we shall see in the next chapter of this study. Khalil's identification
with Paul appears in many places in *Arabia Deserta* (where the apostle
is openly named twice), and Doughty's biblical markings confirm this
interesting association. Near Isa. 59:17—"For he put on righteousness
as a breastplate, and an helmet of salvation upon his head; and he put
on the garments of vengeance for clothing, and was clad with zeal as

a cloak"—Doughty writes "so Paul" in the margin. He also puts "so Paul" near Dan. 10:7, underlining "the men that were with me saw not the vision" and so emphasizing Paul's lone role. In Galatians, Doughty gives us even closer evidence of his identity with Paul, going so far as to criticize Paul's actions and statements as not being zealous enough! Thus Gal. 2:2, which tells of Paul's use of subterfuge in preaching his doctrines to people "of reputation," has an exclamation mark: Khalil is always totally outspoken in Arabia, even when this is dangerous, and makes it a part of his credo as "world-wanderer" never to hide the truth as Paul apparently did sometimes. And in Gal. 2:5, "To whom we gave place by subjection, no, not for an hour; that the truth of the gospel might continue with you," Doughty underlines the word "subjection" and writes "meekness but not subjection." This comment indicates his own understanding of the Pauline creed of zealous humility—rather than "subjection"—that Khalil practices and preaches in *Arabia Deserta.*

As author, Doughty also feels the identification with Paul strongly, for he tells us in the first preface that "The book is not milk for babes," an undoubted paraphrase of 1 Cor. 3:1–2, where Paul says, "And I, brethren, could not speak unto you as unto spiritual, but as unto carnal, even as unto babes in Christ. I have fed you with milk, and not with meat: for hitherto ye were not able to bear it, neither yet now are ye able." Just as Doughty the author preaches a special creed to the reader, so he also felt as Khalil that the Arabs needed preaching to about their human relationships. Near James 3:9, "Therewith bless we God, even the Father; and therewith curse we men, which are made after the similitude of God," he writes "Arabs." In *Arabia Deserta,* we read of the Beduin "their mouths full of cursing and lies and prayers" (II, 558). He also writes "slaves" near Rev. 18:13 which tells how commerce in goods and slaves in Babylon will be destroyed, thus echoing his own class disdain for trade and Victorian hatred of slavery which Khalil preaches to the Arabs on more than one occasion. If we take this evidence as a whole, we see plainly the depth to which Christianity and biblical romanticism penetrated Doughty's own soul as Khalil and as author, as well as his basic humanity; rather than an "agnostic Humanitarian," he is more accurately seen as a deeply Christian humanitarian full of the prejudices of his period.

In addition to the antiquarian influence of the Old Testament and the spiritual influence of the New, we have the explicitly literary example of the Bible. When Doughty underlines part of Hos. 4:3, "every one that dwelleth therein shall languish" and writes "desert" near it, he testifies to the justice of biblical poetic description. Similarly, in Num. 13:32 the phrase "is a land that eateth up the inhabitants thereof" is underlined. Job, the Song of Songs, and the Major and Minor Prophets—taken together, perhaps the most poetic group of biblical books—have heavy underlinings, and at Jer. 20:14 Doughty writes "from Job," testifying to his familiarity with that book. When he underlines the striking phrase "Ancient of days" no less than three times in Daniel (7:9, 7:13, 7:22) and "hammer of the whole earth" (with exclamation mark) in Jer. 50:23, we may be sure he has done so because of simple literary delight. We are not surprised when we find many reminiscences of biblical phrases embedded directly in *Arabia Deserta's* sentences. One prominent example is the underlined "and I will make your heaven as iron, and your earth as brass" from Lev. 26:19 that comes into *Arabia Deserta* beautifully as "the Arabian heaven is burning brass above their heads, and the sand as glowing coals under their weary feet" (I, 79).

This last quotation from *Arabia Deserta* displays a deeper biblical influence on Doughty than mere borrowing and paraphrasing. As Annette McCormick has pointed out, the English translations of the Bible actually supply Doughty with the parallel structure of most of the sentences in his book.[16] Both the fragment from Leviticus quoted above and Doughty's imitation of it consist of two balanced halves whose contrast makes them poetically beautiful. Furthermore, Doughty's frequently noticed lack of connectives between major parts of sentences becomes explainable as a remarkably successful imitation of ancient Hebrew poetic juxtaposition, rather than an eccentric or failed lack of English subordination, according to McCormick. Such a sentence as "There was a great stillness in all their camp; these were the last hours of repose" (I, 6) becomes not stylistic eccentricity, but successful rendering of biblical parallelism as Doughty understood it. And this rhythm of parallelism felt throughout his book accounts for much of its biblical tone, especially in combination with the syntax of spoken Arabic which Doughty frequently employs, as Walt Taylor has pointed out,[17] and which has much in common with Hebrew syntax.

We see that the influence of the Bible on *Arabia Deserta* cannot be overestimated. It provided the basic impetus for the travels, the St. Paul role for Khalil to model himself upon, and finally the very rhythm of thought and speech of Doughty's neo-biblical testament.

C Literary Influences

Outside of the Bible itself, the most obvious influences on Doughty remain Chaucer and Spenser, as he tells us in the second preface by calling himself "a disciple of the divine Muse of Spenser and Venerable Chaucer" and by including a few lines from these poets—in Chaucer's case reproducing the very black-letter print of his 1687 edition—in *Arabia Deserta*. Barker Fairley has shown that Spenser's example was confined largely to the idea of moral quest and vague ambience rather than to much specific stylistic device outside of many individual borrowed words. Chaucer's influence is much more pervasive. In addition to a reinforcement of the pilgrimage idea seen also in Spenser's *Faerie Queen*, Doughty's reading of the *Canterbury Tales* led him to a medieval view of his characters and to Chaucerian touches of style. Thus, Ibrahim becomes one of the "young franklins" of Aneyza (II, 460). Among the pilgrims of the very Chaucerian opening *Háj* or pilgrimage section of *Arabia Deserta* we notice a "yellow-haired young derwîsh, the best minstrel of them all; with the rest of his breath he laughed and cracked and would hail me cheerfully in the best Arabic that he could" (I, 5) as if he had stepped out of Chaucer's prologue. Doughty's narrator's statement about Mohammed Mejelly, the sheikh of Kerak, might have been spoken by the oblique, half-ironic narrator of the prologue of the *Canterbury Tales:* "Mohammed, cock of this hill, of a haughty Arabian beauty, is, they say, a trembler in the field; better him were to comb his beard delicately in a pedlar's glass with his wives at home, than show his fine skin to flying lead and their speary warfare" (I, 25). The chivalric tone and parallelism of the following passage reads like a description of both Chaucer's and Spenser's knights shorn of armor: "His fellows rode with naked legs and unshod upon their beautiful mares' bare backs, the halter in one hand, and the long balanced lance, wavering upon the shoulder, in the other" (I, 30).

The metaphors in the pilgrimage section have a homely, medieval air: "I heard with discomfort of mind their hourly squabbling, as it were rats in a tub, with loud wrangling over every trifle as of fiends in the end of the world. It is a proverb here, that a man will slay the son of his mother for an old shoe leather" (I, 34). Doughty's "chuck! chuck!" (I, 42) to describe partridges' cries reminds us of medieval and Elizabethan lyrics, as does this Phoenix-like passage: "The Syrian lark rose up with flickering wings from this desolate soil, singing before the sun" (I, 47). We think of Chaucer immediately when we read "so gallantly rode chanticleer aloft, in a chain and pair of scarlet jesses" (I, 70), and again when the narrator tells of Mohammed Said "Of most robust pith he was" (I, 74), or when Haj Nejm is made to say "'And wot you why . . . my heart is ever green'" (I, 89). To the six literary modes described in chapter 4 of this study, we can add the Chaucerian narrative of the opening section, or prologue, of *Arabia Deserta*.

In addition to the traces of Chaucer and Spenser, scholars have stressed Doughty's debt to the authors whom he read in the Bodleian Library in 1868–1870. Thus, Annette McCormick attempts to trace the Elizabethan travel writer Hackluyt's influence on Doughty with disappointingly modest results.[18] Others may point to the Elizabethan plays, the Gavin Douglas Scots translation of the *Aeneid*, or to various Anglo-Saxon and theological works listed by Hogarth, to which we can add the Gonville and Caius collection's heavily annotated Italian translation of the *Odyssey*, Erasmus, Latimer, classical Latin authors, anonymous writers of medieval lyrics, and Tyndall, Wycliff, and Cranmer and assorted language dictionaries. The location of specific traces of these works in his sentences and phrases is an amusing academic game, but perhaps more important is the realization of the *total* result of this reading on Doughty's vision. For Doughty's antiquarian literary reading results in the almost medieval roguery, nobility, and saintliness that *Arabia Deserta*'s hero and his opponents display. This description of Zeyd, for instance, owes not a little to Doughty's "chivalric" researches: "Stern were the withered looks of his black visage and pricking sheykhly upon the mare to his endeavour, with the long wavering lance upon his virile shoulder, and the Ishmaelite side-locks flying backward in the wind, the son of Sbeychan seemed a martial figure" (I, 518). Doughty actually saw the Arabs with the eyes of Spenser and Chaucer.

But Doughty's antiquarianism, though of undeniable importance, can be overemphasized. What strikes the critic today is the close similarity of *Arabia Deserta* and other works of the aesthetic movement. Although Doughty insisted that he did not read his contemporaries, and was ignorant of Hardy's name, his antiquarian interest matches that of the Pre-Raphaelites for instance and results in a very similar kind of art. No man lives in a vacuum, and the same basic force— namely, disgust with industrial civilization—acting on Doughty consciously or subconsciously, was impelling his contemporaries to revive past styles.

William Rogers correctly stresses Doughty's close relationship in spirit to his own, rather than past, periods:

There are many similarities aligning Doughty, not with travel writers, but with the literary artists of later Victorian years. Although he wrote in deliberate ignorance of contemporary poets, dramatists, and novelists, his intense concern with stylistic perfection sets him firmly in the ambience of the aesthetic movement. His professed alignment with the tradition of Chaucer and Spenser, while circumventing the stylistic heritage of the Romantics, suggests the similar effort of G. M. Hopkins. . . . His patriotism and consequent fascination with English origins are akin to those of Rudyard Kipling. . . . His stark vision of Arabia has points of contact with Wells's *The Time Machine*—a prophetic book that cuts through Victorian optimism and presents an unsettling vision of a future become nightmare and finally exhaustion and emptiness.[19]

Rogers's citation of Wells's science fiction fits the minor poetry more precisely than it does *Arabia Deserta*, as we shall see in the sixth chapter of this study, but he makes an important point in this quotation. We have only to remember that *Arabia Deserta* was one of William Morris's most beloved books toward the end of his life, and that Edward Burne-Jones spent six months savoring it, to realize how closely in touch with its period it really is.

To Rogers's basic suggestion of parallels, we can add that although Doughty lacks the introspective, fantasy, and antiscience elements of Pre-Raphaelite painting and writing, he shares its nostalgia for the medieval period, for the distant and exotic, its religious enthusiasm, its desire for social reform, and its interest in the textured look. We need think only of Morris's and Burne-Jones's Kelmscott Chaucer and the arabesque, intertwined tapestries of Webb and Morris to understand that Doughty's rich prose possibly owes just as much or more to medieval European pictorial patterns as to the interlaced, abstract Koranic inscriptions that he saw on mosque domes during his travels.

John Hunt delineates Victorian and Pre-Raphaelite characteristics which match Doughty's concerns perfectly: (1) "Medieval and religious enthusiasms seem to go alongside a missionary zeal to reform the age . . ."; (2) among the Pre-Raphaelites there was an attempt to directly assume the themes and dialects of the past; (3) the early Pre-Raphaelites had an intense concern with precise factual description of "indiscriminate detail"; and (4) Victorians generally insisted on mak-

ing Jesus' life and teaching more tangible and actual.[20] Thus, Khalil
enters directly into the living biblical world in order to prove to us that
Christianity *works* in a confrontation with hostile forces, and Doughty
seeks to transform his intensely detailed account of the men and elements of Arabia into a kind of Bible designed to rekindle Victorian
linguistic patriotism and religious belief.

Like every master, Doughty represents a variation on the basic interests of his period. So he adds Elizabethan enthusiasms to medieval and
earlier tendencies and concentrates on the linguistic sphere for reform.
But even his concern with the English language fits his age, as Hugh
Kenner points out:

Mid-19th-century England abounded in amiable enthusiasts for Saxon
roots. . . . Bridges (who said of the old words "We'll get 'em all *back*")
admired Doughty. . . . Doughty in turn was indebted to the *Speechcraft* (i.e.
Grammar) of William Barnes, who proposed *sunprint* or *flameprint* to
replace *photograph*. . . . [21]

Doughty's art for art's sake prose style, which makes no concessions to
popularity and caused him difficulty in finding a publisher, also
reminds us of the work and attitudes of Pater, Ruskin, and Morris.
Arabia Deserta's stylistic experiment is so pronounced that it transforms already exotic content into a romance—despite the book's factual accuracy—no less (but no more) fantastic than Morris's long sagas.
Doughty's book, far from an anomaly, remains a brilliantly novel variation on the tradition of its own age.

II *Composition*

Doughty the author displays the same obsessive secrecy about his
processes of composition as he does when refusing to grant us a close
glimpse of Khalil's inner workings in *Arabia Deserta*. He burned the
manuscript of the book in his garden, giving as an excuse the thought
that it was of no value,[22] and never answered T. E. Lawrence's query
about the relationship of his notebooks—which he kept and sold to the
Fitzwilliam Museum—to the finished product.[23] By destroying the
manuscript, he has deprived us of sure knowledge of the relationship
between fact, memory, and shaping art and the development of his
great style. Only hints about these matters can be gleaned from the
thirteen nearly illegible manuscript travel notebooks, which include a

diary, all in the Fitzwilliam Museum, and from the boxes of "word notes" available at the Gonville and Caius Library. But these sources indicate clearly that *Arabia Deserta* depends as much on art and memory as on its author's actual travel notes and word jottings.

D. G. Hogarth's brilliant work on the notebooks in his *Life* (not the least of which remains his deciphering of Doughty's admittedly impossible handwriting), can be summarized in four points: (1) A certain amount of Doughty's diary itself relies on memory of past events, as when at Kheybar on 30 December 1877 he wrote fourteen pages including all his experiences from 28 November until that date. (2) Doughty had to rely greatly on memory when writing his manuscript of *Arabia Deserta* from the diary, because in the diary he sometimes condensed days or even weeks into a very small space, as when everything that happened to him at Kheybar in the two and a half months after 30 December 1877 is given only one half a diary page. The diary contains a very full outline of some incidents, including dialogue, as when he gives us six crammed pages about Sheikh Salem, but only a very bare skeleton outline of other events, like the three brief sentences he devotes to the Zeyd-Hirfa comedy. (3) The retrospective narrator of *Arabia Deserta* imposes a bitter feeling—not found in some individual diary entries—derived from the whole, complete adventure, even on some early events of the journey. And (4) Doughty thought of publication even while writing parts of his diary because he occasionally revised these stylistically on the spot.

To Hogarth's four main points, which demonstrate in sum just how much Doughty had to rely on his memory for a good part of the tone, dialogue, and details if not basic events in *Arabia Deserta*, we can add a fifth: nowhere in the diary or the other notebooks—or for that matter in the European–North African early diary or his letters—do we find passages or even sentences with anything like the fantastic style of *Arabia Deserta* or with its use of literary modes. For example, the highly colored sentence in which Zeyd and Khalil ride up to the Pasha—"Zeyd greeted with the noble Beduin simplicity in his deep stern tones, and as a landlord in his own country, 'Peace be with thee'" (I, 213)—appears in the diary entry for 14 February 1877 as: "Zeyd greeted good morning in his loud voice." Memory and artistry—who can say which?—have added to *Arabia Deserta*'s account many details absent from the diary original, including a noble tone.

The dialogue detailing Khalil's expulsion from Aneyza shows a similar heightening. Instead of the cadenced speech we get on II, 404–5,

"'But tell me, are there none the better for my medicines in your town?'—'We wish for no medicines.'—'Have I not done well and honestly in Aneyza? answer me, upon your conscience.' *Emir Aly:* 'Well, thou hast.'—'Then what dealing is this?' But he cried, 'Art thou ready? now mount!'" we find in the diary the balder:

"You know at heart that I have done good . . . with my medicines." "We do not wish for your medicines." "tell me honestly if I am not a good man in your sight." "Ay you are so." "Then why deal thus with me." "Make haste . . . mount mount."

We must praise Doughty's incredible diligence in recording—if only briefly—practically every basic event that happened during his journey, and certainly trust his statement about Hirfa, Zeyd's wife, "I have spoken of her as she was absolutely, in my sight, without adding or detracting anything: as I have also of every other person mentioned in the *Arabia Deserta* volumes."[24] But, as Hogarth points out, only three sentences in the diary relate to the Hirfa-Zeyd incident. No man can remember or write down precisely every word spoken and every thought thought during two years of taxing travels. Through memory's gaps can seep imagination or at least colored details, especially when the rememberer of things past has decided to write them up in a style heavily influenced by his own biblical-medieval-Renaissance vision and shapes incidents into tragic, comic, satiric, and other literary modes. These are the lessons of the study of Doughty's notebooks.

The second source of compositional information, the "word notes," consists of a suitcase containing "General Word Notes," a blue box of "*Arabia Deserta* Word Notes," and other boxes of word notes of various Doughty poems. These offer evidence of the intense concern with word choice that forms the groundwork of all Doughty's art. He would carry scraps of paper around with him at all times, perhaps even in Arabia, and jot down as the fancy took him the almost Freudian associations that coalesced in his mind around a given word. Thus, on an individual word note we might find quotations containing the word, synonyms, and related words, sometimes in several languages. When he had collected a number of word notes for different words, he would order the word notes alphabetically, thus constructing his own personal combination thesaurus and quotation dictionary which he would call on while writing a given poem or *Arabia Deserta*, and even continue adding to while writing up a work. When he finished one work, he would put aside the word notes used in that work and begin assembling a new set. All this reminds us of James Murray's compilation of the *Oxford English Dictionary*, which was taking place in the same period, yet another sign of Doughty's relation to his times.

In the "General Word Notes" which Doughty kept in a suitcase because he moved around so much, we find twenty-one alphabetically ordered parcels of word notes, each tied by a white ribbon. If we look at the word note for "accomplish," for instance, we find "compass, achieve, perfect, perform, fulfill, bring to pass" and "to effect" written on it. On the two word notes headed "Arabia Deserta" we find "void waste, swash bucklers, rapine, courses of square stone, outlaw, gaunt hills, hewn in a sandstone cliff, always ailing, this young Absalom," and "Princes of Arabia," all aspects of the desert and even phrases that find their way into *Arabia Deserta*. The "Tempest" slip from the parcel marked "T" contains the words "tornado, hurricane," and "typhoon," along with bits of poetry about storms.

The "*Arabia Deserta* Word Notes" grouped into four main parcels, "A-Fi," "Fi-Kha," "Kh-Ov," and "Ov-W," each containing smaller parcels of slips, offer deeper insight into the making of *Arabia Deserta* than the "General Word Notes," as might be expected. We sometimes find a fuller, even more blunt, view of the Arabs than we get in the book itself. One of the fullest packages of notes, as we would expect from Doughty, is "Fanaticism," where we find the words "it is the old hatred of the uncircumcised, violent, bestial, implacable, this fiendish perversity of mind, jehad." The slip headed "Syrians" and subheaded "Mood here Anger Mens Soul" contains the words "wholly faithless— eyes only for their interest, ingenuous-disingenuous, graceless—inso- lent baseness, treacherous mistrust of other. full of inarticulate covetous desires. . . . Ignorant gravity . . . full of bestiality. boastful levity. . . . Never or rarely well disposed. Corruption of all in office. . . . He is not thy good friend beyond opportunity of self interest and instantly turns upon you. . . . smile or just brazen it out." Despite his "certain preju- dice against all things Semitic" in Hogarth's words,[25] Doughty appears to have actually moderated the views on this slip, perhaps in the inter- est of a more spiritual and humane tone, when it came to writing *Ara- bia Deserta* itself! A slip on "Arabs" however contains a more balanced assessment, with Doughty writing "impetuous—curious—impatient . . . insolent . . . iniquitous . . . ambitious—cheerful railling-liars," and the "Hospitality" slips inform us that "The Arab hospitality is often magnanimous."

The "Christianity" packet contains in addition to the expected positive words the negative "found (impracticable)" and "a sad religion." But our view of Doughty's distaste for the Old Testament spirit and reverence for the New which we discussed in connection with the religious influences acting on him, finds confirmation when we read under "history of Jews" the words "iniquitous, disastrous, irksome, cruel, dreary, savage and barbarous," along with many favorable words about Jesus, all in the "Jesu" parcel.

"Kheybar," "Religio," and "Sinai" have thick batches of slips devoted to them, but the most interesting comments for those concerned with Doughty's artistry are perhaps found in the "Style" set of slips, where he writes "robust simplicity of ancients, reminder of the ancient language, precision, *fall* of the verse rhymes" and "robust fantasy" as a testimony to the qualities of older literature that he reverenced. And the "Desert" parcel contains the stylistically and spiritually evocative "I am miswent, infinite, illimitable, solitudines, inhuman, forlorn, lorn, lone, wild waste moors, desolate, forlaetynsse, dry uplands," and "it is as a pass through the nether world," clear indications of Doughty's feelings as revealed in *Arabia Deserta* itself.

Some of the word notes are actually fragments of larger pages, perhaps early *Arabia Deserta* manuscript forms. In the "Antiquity" group we find a torn page that seems to be echoed in revised form at many points of *Arabia Deserta:*

The Beduwin appear to be Degenerate in Islam for the ancient spirit of their nation. That deadly acquiescence of theirs calling it the will of Allah in the native indolence of their race—climate builds their natural . . . want of union such that they can hardly help themselves at present in any undertaking!

In the word notes as in the notebooks we see Doughty's mind forming the thoughts and sentences out of which *Arabia Deserta* eventually evolved; and we come to appreciate if not actually measure (owing to the destruction of the manuscript) the great artistic journey involved in the process.

Another proof of the extent of this artistic voyage is the time it took. No man merely reporting his travels would have taken so long to work notebooks into literature. He began writing in or around June 1879 and finished the manuscript by May 1883, with some time out for the work of publishing separately his strictly scientific results. Then came the revision of his manuscript and proofs that followed Cambridge University's acceptance of the work on 6 February 1885, and which lasted until July 1887 when he gave the revised proofs to the German scholar Edward Sachau for final checking. Doughty had the expensive habit of altering many things in the proofs, but since only a few sheets remain, we may not trace the details of his changes in any depth. Finally the work was published early in 1888.

Before Cambridge accepted the project Doughty had been turned down by four commercial publishers because of his strange writing style. Even Cambridge wanted the style thoroughly revised by Professor Robertson Smith, but luckily Doughty's artistic obstinacy prevailed. After his physical and literary exertions, the struggle with publishers was terrible and heartbreaking for him but produced at least one great letter which serves as a monument of artistic integrity. When the Royal Geographical Society attempted to edit the text of Doughty's 1883 lecture by putting it into a more contemporary or usual English, he wrote: " . . . as an English scholar I will never submit to have my language of the best times turned into the misery of today—that were unworthy of me."[26]

Doughty's refusal to compromise on style, so similar to Khalil's Christian obstinacy in Arabia, earned him the enthusiastic admiration of one relatively unknown but highly intelligent contemporary, Trelawney Saunders of the map section of the India Office. Saunders writes to Doughty on 9 April 1884, after the R.G.S. gave Doughty trouble about his style, that

Bates showed me yesterday the first page of the proof of your paper with his "corrections." I fought him upon every one of them; for I think the novelty of style delicious, and I could not discover a word that is not capable of a sound defence. I reminded him of Carlyle, although it is an injustice to you to have your style compared with his barbaric dialect. . . . [27]

On 8 July 1884, he comments on Macmillan's failure to accept the book, and then on 18 February 1885, informed of Cambridge's positive decision, writes "See the Conquering Hero comes! I am highly delighted not only at your very gratifying victory but also at the humiliating defeat of the critical quidnuncs, who would reduce writing to one standard, and crush individuality." Saunders has spoken with prescience for all subsequent admirers of Doughty's art. Laborious and painful as the composition and publication of *Arabia Deserta* were, Doughty's work has been justified by time with the status of a world masterpiece, whose nature we will now investigate.

III   *Literary Personae*

At first glance, the narration of the autobiographical *Arabia Deserta* would seem to present no problems. As narrator of the book Doughty always refers to himself as "I" and the Arabs call him "Khalil," exactly as they did in Arabia. What could be more straightforward? But all observers have noticed a certain difference, or distance, between the narrative voice that tells the story and Khalil, the protagonist who acts in it. Barker Fairley explains this felt difference in the following way: "It goes without saying that when Doughty looked back at those extraordinary days, they seemed unbelievably strange to him and that he was unable to work with a complete sense of identity between himself who was writing and the man whose astonishing story he was telling."[28] The distance between the narrator and Khalil the protagonist can be seen in three areas of the text itself. First, "Khalil" is not just any name, a mere phonetic equivalent of "Charles," but a highly symbolic name, meaning "Friend," and referring to Islam's "Friend of God," Abraham (I, 446; II, 614). By continually calling him this, the Arab characters in *Arabia Deserta* transform the protagonist into a kind of allegorical Everyman, thus giving him a quality not found in the narrator's descriptions of him. And, in fact, Khalil as we see him in *Arabia Deserta* is an idealized artistic construct who represents the best in Doughty's personality. Further, we find that Khalil—as in his conversations with Abdullah El Kenneyny in Aneyza—comes out with declarations of universal love and religious tolerance in addition to more prejudiced remarks, while the more bitter and ironic retrospective narrator, who is never of course under social pressure since he is only a voice, never admits Islam to the inner circle of civilized religions and only very rarely or never shows the tolerance that we see in some of Khalil's conversations. Finally, the narrator occasionally offers forward-looking information—as for instance when he mentions the Bombay Jews (II, 127) whom Doughty was to meet only after leaving Arabia—which the Khalil who is limited to knowledge of the present cannot know about. Thus, whether or not he precisely intended this separation between narrative voice and protagonist, Doughty the artist created it, and the reader feels it more and more as the book progresses.

As the use of the term "Doughty the artist" indicates, we find yet another distinction operating in the narrative texture of *Arabia Deserta:* that between the narrative voice, which describes and comments on the characters and action, including Khalil's thoughts, and reports the dialogue, and Doughty the artist, who almost like a novelist controls both Khalil and the narrative voice. It is Doughty the artist who creates the dialogue of the characters, decides which characters will be included in the book, which incidents concerning Khalil and other characters the narrator will report, which words the narrator will use, which qualities of the characters the narrator will stress, when things will happen, where the chapter divisions, illustrations, appendixes, index, and map will be, and speaks directly to us in the prefaces.

D. H. Lawrence noticed the difference between artist and narrator when he commented about Melville that "the artist was so much greater than the man."[29] By this, he meant that Ishmael, Melville's mouthpiece-narrator in *Moby Dick,* is frequently preachy and tiresome and that the book is much more complicated than Ishmael is. As we shall see at greater length in the next chapter, Norman Douglas noted his own shift of sympathy away from Khalil and the narrator and toward the Arab characters during a second reading of *Arabia Deserta* after World War I. It is Doughty the artist, with his conscious and subconscious integrity and desire to respect the "truth" and deep human empathy, who has made this shift of sympathy possible, because he is much "greater" than either the narrator or Khalil. He has put powerful words in the mouths of the Arab characters, and has made the narrator (who strikes us in his dogmatism and moralizing as very much a limited Victorian) include incidents and statements which do not always support his case, even when he thinks they do. In other words, as conscious teller of his tale, Doughty reveals his own Victorian narrowness and limitations; but as deep artist, he has shown much more sympathy and understanding than he consciously knows, and this appears in many ways.

For example, Sirur, Abdullah's lieutenant at Kheybar, is depicted as a stupid and brutal bully in the narrator's report of his actions, the narrator's assessment of those actions, and in Khalil's dialogues with him. But in at least one incident the modern reader will side with Sirur rather than with the narrator and Khalil. Khalil tries to determine the ethnic origins of the people of Kheybar, using his crude, pseudo-scientific nineteenth-century physical anthropology:

Seeing these more Arab-looking, and even copper-coloured village faces, and that some young men here wore their negro locks braided as the Nomads,

I enquired, had they no tradition of their ancestry. They answered me: "We are Jeheyna;—but is there nothing of Kheybar written in your books?"— "Are not the Kheyâbara from the Sudàn?—or from whence have they these lips and noses?" (II, 93–94)

Sirur responds to Khalil's comment about "lips and noses" as follows: "*Sirûr* (with his ribald malice), 'Come up, each of ye people of Umm Kida! and let this wise stranger feel each of your noses (khusshm), and declare to you what ancestry ye be of, and where is every man's natural bêled'" (II, 94). Despite the narrator's obvious intention of denigrating Sirur ("with ribald malice" indicates the narrator's view of Sirur's intentions), the modern reader, knowing the dangers of Khalil's badly based "racial" anthropology, will find Sirur's comments more wise than malicious, or properly malicious. The narrator wants us to take sides against Sirur, but the artist in Doughty has made it possible for us to do the opposite. In Sirur's remarks we feel his justified resentment against the white man's "scientific" racism and perhaps against Khalil's superior tone when uttering "'these lips and noses,'" all of which Doughty the artist has captured perfectly and preserved for the alert reader. Somewhat more obvious examples of the same phenomenon of artist outflanking narrator and Khalil are the well-stated defense of polygamy by the Beduin and Mohammed Ibn Rashid's intelligent suspicion of colonialism, both of which views the characters state powerfully while the narrator and Khalil fail to agree with them.

We can sum up the narrative forces operating in *Arabia Deserta* in the following convenient manner: (1) *Khalil:* The protagonist who acts and speaks and is addressed by other characters in the present, and whose thoughts, actions, and dialogue are reported and described by the narrator. An idealized Everyman version of Doughty's personality. (2) *The narrator:* The highly intelligent but moralistic and prejudiced voice which describes and comments on the characters (including Khalil and his thoughts), and on the action, sometimes looking ahead of it or to a period before it occurred. He also reports and comments on the dialogue. Doughty as conscious Victorian. (3) *Doughty the artist:* The force which created and controls all the elements in the work, of which Khalil and the narrator are only two. He decides on the narrator's tone and thought and the style of the whole work, and precisely what Khalil or another character will say and do, and when they will say or do it. Because of the power he gives them in dialogue, the Arab characters frequently appear in a more favorable light than Khalil and the narrator (who reports the dialogue) think they do. Doughty as conscious and subconscious artist.

Because Doughty the artist is far greater than Doughty the man of his times (whom we see in the narrator's voice), his book becomes capable of continual self-renewal in all circumstances and periods, like any masterpiece. We perceive clearly the narrator's and Khalil's prejudices but can read through these to a greater sympathy with the Arabs and a more complex enjoyment of the book that Doughty the artist has made possible.

While we praise Doughty the artist of *Arabia Deserta* for his human sympathy, we must note that Doughty reveals a very different side of his artistic personality in the poetry, with the possible exception of *Adam Cast Forth*. In *Arabia Deserta*, Doughty had real people to work on, and by portraying them in all their complex detail as they appeared to him he surpassed his own narrow preconceptions of how they should be. The deep artist predominates over the Victorian narrator, as we have seen. Furthermore, Khalil becomes a saint—despite his faults—owing to his sufferings. If we wish to translate Doughty's artistic personality in *Arabia Deserta* somewhat simplistically, we can say that the book on the whole reveals his "masochistic" side, and that it is by far his best side. Desert sufferings seem to have liberated in him unknown artistic depths of sympathy not just for Khalil, but for the Arabs as well.

In the poetry, on the other hand, we find an overt sadism and almost fanatic chauvinism which can never sympathize with the perceived enemies of England, and which results in too many very bloody battle scenes in *Dawn in Britain* and the extremity of child sacrifice for Britain's sake in *The Cliffs*. It is as if only the moralizing and prejudiced narrator of *Arabia Deserta*, pushed to an extreme, exists in the characters, action, and speaker's voice of the poetry, without the qualifying greatness of the artist of *Arabia Deserta*. Only in *Adam Cast Forth*, where Doughty recapitulates his desert sufferings, do we feel a truly human note. In the rest of the poetry, where he creates his own fictional or semihistorical beings without deep autobiographical connections, the result is either black and white stereotyping and wooden characters, or vapid abstractions. In short, in *Arabia Deserta*, Doughty reaches subconscious artistic depths of his personality, while in the poetry he remains the conscious, boring, and simpleminded Victorian patriot who addresses us directly through speaker's voice and characters as well. The distinction between the three narrative elements of

Arabia Deserta and the difference between *Arabia Deserta* and the poetry noted here are worth keeping in mind, and we will do so throughout this book. However, these are only literary distinctions used to facilitate precise discussion of the works, and we should always remember that they represent only different aspects of the man Charles Montagu Doughty, himself.

IV *Genre*

For all its apparent strangeness, *Travels in Arabia Deserta* can be precisely classified—and therefore correctly understood and evaluated—as an oratorical autobiography of travel. We arrive at this last term by combining complementary phrases of D. G. Hogarth and William Howarth. Hogarth's phrase "autobiography of travel" accurately characterizes Doughty's and other artistic travel books, which are typically "about" their authors at least as much as they illuminate the places the authors visited. Howarth's phrase "autobiography as oratory" refers to a specific major subgenre of autobiography, or literary self-portraiture, which he has discovered.[30]

An "oratorical"—as opposed to a "dramatic" or "poetic"—autobiography is basically a work in which a sympathetic narrator recounts from a distance and in a very sermonlike rhetorical style, the adventures of a protagonist who is used to illustrate a moral point. The protagonist may be portrayed comically—like the respective heroes Henry Adams and Norman Mailer of *The Education of Henry Adams* and *The Armies of the Night*, both oratorical autobiographies—or seriously, as Khalil is.

Doughty's book fits Howarth's category well. In the last section of this chapter, we noticed a distance between *Arabia Deserta*'s narrator and protagonist. In the next chapter, we will see that the sympathetic but distanced narrator portrays Khalil as a saint worth emulating despite his faults in order to prove that the Christian virtues of self-renunciation and love even of enemies actually *work* when tested in an extreme way, and also that an Englishman armed with only modern science and English integrity can overcome all obstacles. Thus *Arabia Deserta* was consciously intended as a very ideological moral work whose main purpose is to serve as a spiritual testament of revived Christianity and British patriotism.

The book's rhetorical style also fits Howarth's description of the features of the oratorical autobiography. Doughty writes some of the most highly developed prose in the whole of English literature, and it owes a great deal to religious influences as we have seen. Doughty's understanding of the rhythms of English Bible translations, the Arabic speech which resembles biblical Hebrew for him, and the religious tracts of Wycliff, Cranmer, and Bunyan which he loved to read, all play their part. He uses the devices of the very "sermonlike" style that results from these influences to manipulate the reader into seeing Khalil's story as timeless, morally transcending all ages. Doughty also hoped that his rhetorical style would refresh what he considered the decayed English language of his contemporaries, another ideological aspect of his book. So its style, like its distance between narrator and protagonist and its use of the protagonist to prove a moral point, demonstrates *Arabia Deserta*'s status as an *oratorical* autobiography of travel. It remains for us now to examine this style through which Doughty shatters the reader's mundane world and substitutes for it a much more exotic grammar of language and experience.

V *Stylistic Goals*

Doughty structures his literary recapitulation of his meandering journey according to successively different literary modes which reflect to some degree the development of his own sensibility in the course of his travels. The lighthearted Chaucerian narrative of the opening *Hâj* section leads to the fabulous Eastern narrative of the *kella* at Medain Salih, with its implicit warning against mistaking Arabian illusions for reality; then the free, simple comedy of the Zeyd-Hirfa "romance" gives way to the high tragedy of Mohammed Ibn Rashid and the dark Gothic of the Kheybar episode; and the bitter satire of manners of the Aneyza section, which reflects Khalil's disillusionment with Arabic culture at this point, leads to the climactic adventure writing of sheer physical survival in Khalil's struggle against Salem and Fheyd, and an ironic denouement.

But if we look within each of these larger sections of the book to each individual page, we will find abrupt and unstructured leaps of subject matter and tone, without the slightest transition: "As for me who write, I pray that nothing be looked for in this book but the seeing of an hungry man and the telling of a most weary man; for the rest the sun made me an Arab, but never warped me to Orientalism. Highland Arabia is not all sand; it is dry earth, nearly without sprinkling of the rains" (I, 56). Thus, although we can maintain that Doughty has suc-

ceeded in at least loosely structuring large episodes and providing some
development in mood through the book as a whole, we can make no
such claim for given pages within those episodes. What we do find on
every page, however, are highly structured sentences and passages,
sometimes amounting to a few paragraphs. Doughty remains always
the artist of the sentence, occasionally the artist of the paragraph,
rarely or never the artist of several pages, and clearly the artist of all
larger scenes and episodes. In chapter 4 we will deal with his means of
dramatic structuring of the larger episodes. Now we will concentrate
on the pervasive artistry of the sentence and paragraph—in short, on
his style, which has aroused so much praise and blame.

Part of the "blame" accruing to *Arabia Deserta*'s style derives from
its supposed lack of readability owing to the use of Arabic and older
English words. But as Walt Taylor has pointed out, Doughty usually
carefully defines a new Arabic word when it first appears, and there-
after relies, quite reasonably, on the reader's memory. He has also provided an admirable glossary to help refresh flagging memory. The
serious reader quickly learns that Doughty's use of Arabic words as a
means of attempting to create an authentic atmosphere offers very little actual obstacle after a certain number of pages, which varies in the
case of each reader, but is rarely more than thirty or forty.

Barker Fairley and especially Anne Treneer have worked on
Doughty's older English words, revealing their origins and, where necessary, precise (and forgotten) meanings. But here again the earnest
reader will not find an occasional—perhaps one every several paragraphs—Anglo-Saxon, Elizabethan, or for that matter scientific-tech-
nical word particularly distressing. The actual difficulty of reading
Arabia Deserta has been greatly exaggerated. The truth is that very
few people today are ready to read one thousand pages of *any* style,
even the most obvious.

Far more important than the perhaps overstressed philological
aspects of Doughty's individual words and the supposed difficulty they
create for readers is the use he puts them to in combination with other
words, and the effect of the *whole* on the reader's sensibility. *Arabia
Deserta* is not a textbook of Old, Middle, or Renaissance English or
Arabic-English correspondences, but a living literary work written in
Doughty's unique combination of these elements and others. If it can
be demonstrated that his special diction, syntax, and rhythms have in
each case a specific literary purpose and influence on the reader attain-
able by no other combination of words, then complaints like G. M.

Hopkins's against the "archaism" of *Arabia Deserta* (which he had not read and which is not so far removed from his own neo-medieval aesthetic), go by the wayside. For what remains ultimately important about any style is not how it fits into a preconceived ideology about what style should or should not be, but whether or not it *works* by succeeding in creating a special and attractive world for the reader to inhabit, and in conveying the atmosphere of the content of the work.

Before we see exactly how Doughty's style succeeds in this way, perhaps we should note the great similarity between Doughty's stylistic *goals* and those of his period. In the famous preface to *The Nigger of the Narcissus*, which appeared just ten years after Doughty's book, in 1898, Conrad states that: "My task which I am trying to achieve is, by the power of the written word to make you hear, to make you feel— it is, before all, to make you *see*. That—and no more, and it is everything."[31] In the second preface to *Arabia Deserta* Doughty writes: "The haps that befel me are narrated in these volumes: wherein I have set down, that which I saw with my eyes, and heard with my ears and thought with my heart, neither more or less" (xii). And in the third preface he transfers these sense perceptions from writer to reader: "While the like phrases of their nearly-allied and not less ancient speech, are sounding in our ears, and their like customs, come down from antiquity, are continued before our eyes; we almost feel ourselves carried back to the days of the nomad Hebrew Patriarchs. . ." (xvi). The desire to create a sensory experience for the reader is common, perhaps uncannily so, to both statements. Like Conrad, Doughty wanted to make his experience live, and that desire dictated the unusual style which for him was the only way to capture his Eastern experience honestly, directly, and personally. Doughty wants nothing less than to put us into Arabia so that we hear, smell, see, and feel it; and he believes that only his "exotic" style can fully recapture his exotic experience. A paraphrase of the first sentence of *Arabia Deserta* and then analyses of passages drawn from each of the six major scenes reveal the precise ways in which Doughty's style works on the reader to make him see and hear according to Doughty's wishes, as well as the reasons for those wishes.

VI   The First Sentence

From the very beginning of the famous first sentence of *Arabia Deserta*, Doughty through the narrator's voice manages to frustrate

normal patterns of thought and assault the reader's expectations of language itself, as well as to toy with his notions of time and space:

A new voice hailed me of an old friend when, first returned from the Peninsula, I paced again in that long street of Damascus which is called Straight;
and suddenly taking me wondering by the hand "Tell me (said he), since
thou art here again in the peace and assurance of Ullah, and whilst we walk,
as in the former years, toward the new blossoming orchards, full of the sweet
spring as the garden of God, what moved thee, or how couldst thou take such
journeys into the fanatic Arabia?" (I, 1)

Only a more normal paraphrase of this first great sentence will demonstrate clearly just how unusual it is:

The new voice of an old friend hailed me as I was pacing in the Straight
Street of Damascus after my return from the Arabian Peninsula. Suddenly
grasping my hand in wonder, my friend asked, "Now that you are back here
under God's protection in a safe place and we are walking as we used to in
past years toward the blossoming orchards that are as fresh as Eden, maybe
you could tell my why and how you managed to travel into that fanatic
area?"

This paraphrase, faulty as all paraphrases of poetic prose must inevitably be, lacks the following features of Doughty's original: (1) The
syntax that, like a good painting's leading of the eye, focuses the
reader's attention on the new voice, the pacing, the name "Straight,"
the friend's "'Tell me,'" and "'fanatic Arabia.'" In the paraphrase, the
friend's question approximates English directness rather than the perfumed intricacies of Arabic speech of the original. (2) The Swinbur-
nean orchestration of vowels and consonants that turns Damascus into
an illusory paradise full of never-ending balm and unction and reproduces to some degree the deep sounds of Arabic. (3) The sense of intimacy between Khalil and his friend created by the archaic familiar
forms "thou" and "thee." (4) The periodic suspense of the original
which hovers over the sentence until the last few phrases. (5) The geographical mystery of "the Peninsula" which remained undefined until
"'fanatic Arabia'" in the original. That clichéd but powerful chord is
gone as well. (6) The heavy use of parallelism that reminds the reader
of biblical rhythms in a subliminal way.

We see clearly that Doughty the artist's chosen syntax, diction, and
rhythm create a special world of their own unattainable by other
arrangements and choice of words and far more interesting and

appealing than more "normal" utterance. Doughty moves us into another cultural realm and we go along with him; and his style works like no other could have, especially in this first sentence, to suggest the exoticism, illusive quality of time and space, richness, danger, and mystery of Arabia for Doughty, which we see mirrored in the work as a whole.

VII   Stylistic Registers

Since Doughty's devices of inversion, parallelism, periodicity, alliteration, older English diction, Arabic diction and rhythms, striking metaphors, and vowel orchestration remain present throughout the book's twelve hundred pages in both the narrator's statements and the characters' dialogues (a fantastic feat of sustained artistry in itself), we are perhaps not justified in speaking of many completely different styles in *Arabia Deserta*, as we are in the case of T. E. Lawrence's *Seven Pillars of Wisdom*, for instance.[32] But we should notice that by varying the amounts of each of these devices in given passages, Doughty is able to achieve a wide variety of tone that saves his prose from monotonous uniformity. The tonal variation that the reader hears in moving from scene to scene or from the narrator to Khalil's, Mohammed Ibn Rashid's, or other Arabic-speaking character's dialogue, is perhaps best understood in terms of the late nineteenth-century analogy between style and music, thus proving once again that Doughty is an artist of his time. Seen in these terms, *Arabia Deserta*'s style ranges from an utterance in which melodious sound and rhythm are very heavily employed to enhance mood and meaning to sentences in which sound is deliberately ugly or not very important at all. In each case, Doughty has a reason for what he is doing. The following chart— a stylistic table arranged in decreasing levels of melodiousness—clarifies Doughty's tonal range:

1. *Musical:* Sound very important to meaning. Use of almost all devices to project a mood.
2. *Exotic:* Stress on musical sounds of spoken Arabic. Accurate translation of Arabisms into English, but creates strange impression in a Western reader. Projects us into the other culture sensorily.
3. *Mixed:* Arabic rhythms and diction deliberately contrasted with narrator's more sober "English" utterance to create ironic effect.
4. *Dissonant:* Use of ugly sounds, including a more plain Arabic expression, to criticize and deflate rather than enhance subject.

5. *Direct:* Adventure writing in some passages, relying on suspenseful periodicity, monosyllabic words, narrative directness, lack of Arabic words and rhythms. Focuses reader on very immediate dangers in unobtrusive style.

6. *Plain:* Factual description. Usual syntax, no assonance or alliteration. Sound does not contribute to meaning.

By examining closely small samples of Doughty's style, ranging from a highly melodious register 1 passage through a relatively plain register 6 passage, we learn how Doughty influences the reader through sound and see how flexible an instrument *Arabia Deserta*'s style can be.

A   Register 1: Musical

We mounted in the morrow twilight; but long after daybreak the heavens seemed shut over us, as a tomb, with gloomy clouds. We were engaged in the horrid lava beds; and were very oftentimes at fault among sharp shelves, or finding before us precipitous places. The vulcanic field is a stony flood which has stiffened; long rolling heads, like horse-manes, of those slaggy waves ride and over-ride the rest: and as they are risen they stand petrified, many being sharply split lengthwise, and the hollow laps are partly fallen down in vast shells and in ruinous heaps as of massy masonry. (II, 71)

The narrator's description reflects Khalil's apprehensions about what he will find later in Kheybar; it is a subjective projection of personality and mood, rather than an "objective" account, like so many other landscapes in *Arabia Deserta*. Instead of Arabic language exoticism, which the narrator frequently employs in his statements, we have the exotic technical language of geology: slaggy, laps. But these words are woven into a dense, pronounced fabric of prose which reflects the content of the passage, and therefore do not obtrude.

We see in this passage particularly why Doughty could write Hogarth that he conceived of *Arabia Deserta* as a poem and "only nominally prose."[33] In the first sentence, we have an orchestration of *o* and *s* sounds, and alliterations on the letter *m*, all of which accentuate the gloomy tomblike atmosphere in the manner of Poe. In the second sentence, the alliterations "sharp shelves" and "precipitous places" accentuate the content. The final *m* alliterations of the last sentence bring us back to the heavy, gloomy feeling of the first sentence, thus unifying the passage through sound.

The heavy use of parallelism in all parts of the passage underlines the content, as Doughty piles up heaps of massy phrases to match the "massy masonry" the narrator has been describing. The rhythmic repetition of "ride and over-ride" and all the *r* alliterations that rise in pitch as the third sentence progresses, reinforce through sound the simile of the wild horses. The horses progressively "rise" only to be frozen in motion, and some even fall back into a "ruinous" tumbled-down condition by the end of the sentence. It is as if we watch the heads of horses on a merry-go-round that has been stopped suddenly. Doughty has taken accurate and precise geological description and turned it into an unforgettable landscape painting with style and force. We have a great romantic picture of a ruined land, which is properly compared to the masonry of a ruined house, the action of galloping horses, and an arrested flood. Delacroix or Max Ernst are the only painters equal to the task of portraying the tremendous, arrested motion and organic, sealike power of this ruined landscape.

B Register 2: Exotic

I saluted the Emir, *Salaam aleyk.*—No answer: then I greeted Hamûd and Sleymàn, now of friendly acquaintance, in the same words, and with *aleykom es-salaam* they hailed me smiling comfortably again. One showed me to a place where I should sit down before the Emir, who said shortly "From whence?"—"From my makhzan."—'And what found I there to do all the day, ha! and what had I seen in the time of my being at Hâyil, was it well?' When the Prince said, "Khalîl!" I should have responded in their manner *Aunak* or *Labbeyk* or *Tawîl el-Ummr*, "O Long-of-age! and what is thy sweet will?" but feeling as an European among these light-tongued Asiatics, and full of mortal weariness, I kept silence. So the Emir, who had not responded to my salutation, turned abruptly to ask Hamûd and Sleymàn: *Má yarúdd?* 'how! he returns not one's word who speaks with him?' Hamûd responded kindly for me, 'He could not tell, it might be Khalîl is tired.' I answered after the pause, "I am lately arrived in this place, but *aghrûty*, I suppose it is very well." (II, 11–12)

The narrator reports precisely each small detail of the Emir Mohammed Ibn Rashid's imperious manner and tone, Hamud's softer, kinder expression, and Khalil's prophetlike bluntness of speech. In this "translated" Arabic dialogue, we hear the lively and inverted rhythm of Arabic speech, even in the indirect quotations (indicated by single rather than double quotation marks). The speaker of Hebrew no less than the Arabic speaker testifies to the true rhythm of "'And what found I there to do all the day, ha! and what had I seen in the time of my being at Hâyil, was it well?'" If we translate this statement into Hebrew and write it phonetically, the precision of Doughty's ear will immediately become apparent: "Uma matzati (lenachon) laasot sham kol hayom, ha! uma raiti bizman heyoti behaiyl, haya ze tov?" In his *For Whom the Bell Tolls, The Sun Also Rises,* and *The Old Man and the Sea,* Hemingway continually and unashamedly attempts the same thing as Doughty does in his Arabic translations by finding English equivalents for French and Spanish rhythms, phrases, and sentences. But the fact that Doughty deals with a non-Western culture and a language which reminds him of biblical parallelism accounts for a far greater complexity of result than in Hemingway's case, as does Doughty's overt use of Arabic words and his preference for older English diction and rhythms. Although we can understand exactly what is being said for the most part (some of the Arabic words are not translated in the glossary, but *are* translated elsewhere in the text, as *Labbeyk,* II, 481), know that Doughty reproduces Arabic speech amazingly well, and notice that the characterization that emerges from this passage is extremely subtle, a fascinating tone of exoticism for the Western reader unacquainted with Semitic languages results from the sheer and different (for him) *music* of Arabic diction and rhythms. Doughty through his narrator forces us to *listen* to a different culture and thereby experience its mental grammar. Although he tells us of Khalil's disapproval of "light tongued Asiatics," the narrator's own voice is more inverted than usual to match the rhythms of the Arabic dialogue he has been reporting.

C   *Register 3: Mixed*

Once we heard a strange noise in the hollow of our cavern upward. Doolan, who came with us, afterward boasted "We had all heard, wellah, the bogle, *ghrûl,* ay, and even the incredulous son-of-his-uncle Khalîl:" but I thought it only a rumble in the empty body of Wady's starveling greyhound, for which we had no water and almost not a crumb to cast, and that lay fainting above us. (I, 131)

In the Medain Salih *kella* sequence, Doughty—through his narrator—wants to show us that nothing is quite what the Arabs say it is. Doolan's vocal rhythms, emphases, and strange words all contrast sharply with the down-to-earth narrator's utterance to which they are paralleled. Arabic speech appears animated and inflated by interjections of conviction and adjectives as even the truly incredulous Khalil is said to have witnessed the exotic "*ghrûl*," or specter—only to be totally punctured by the narrator's immediate report in the most sober and normal language, free of Arabic's heightened emphases, that Khalil heard no such thing.

D Register 4: Dissonant

The peasant divine looked up more mildly, yet would he not hold speech with one of the heathen; but leaning over to the negro Aly, who brought me hither, he charged him, in a small dying voice, to ask, 'Had the Nasrâny a remedy for the emerods?'—the negro shouted these words to the company! "It sufficeth," responded the morose pedant; and settling his leathern chaps his dunghill spirit reverted to her wingless contemplation, at the gates of the Meccàwy's paradise.—In such religious dotage we perceive no aspect of the Truth! which is so of kin to our better nature that we should know her, even through a rent of her veil, as the young one knows his mother. (II, 377–78)

In the Aneyza episode, an intolerant and ignorant Moslem refuses to speak directly to the "heathen" physician Khalil, even as he begs him for medicines. Ugly and dissonant sound becomes the main hinge of the narrator's bitter irony against the "divine." The man's "small dying" voice is cowardly and has none of the exotic rhythm, diction, and therefore beauty of the Arabic speech we heard in the Ibn Rashid or Doolan incidents quoted above: "'Had the Nasrâny a remedy for the emerods?'" His actual complaint, hemorrhoids, is comic in a vulgar and deflating way, and the detail of Aly's shouting out the man's question "to the company" brings out incongruously and therefore ironically the weakness of the man's own voice and spirit. Now the narrator becomes more heavy-handed in his irony, calling the Moslem a "morose pedant" (a description which matches the man's stuffy "'It sufficeth'"), and referring to his "leathern chaps" (jaws, but implies backside), "dunghill spirit," and "wingless contemplation." "Dunghill" remains one of the narrator's favorite words of abuse, and is a polite but ugly-sounding euphemism for "*khára*" or "shit," which Doughty allows the narrator to mention only in Arabic, never in English, according to Victorian conventions, translating it only as "draffe, or worse." The divine's Arabic speech, like his backside, is painfully constricted, unlike the more beautiful Arabic we have heard.

But there is even more soundplay in this passage. The controlling metaphor is that of thought which never takes wing ("wingless contemplation") and reminds us of the narrator's earlier dictum, "The Semites are like to a man sitting in a cloaca to the eyes, and whose brows touch heaven" (I, 56), but without the redeeming touching of heaven. The bird metaphor is reinforced by a subtle soundplay. The choice of the word "Meccàwy's" here, instead of a more usual and melodious word for Moslem, occurs because of its ugly (and accented) birdlike sound, "caw," which recalls a crow rather than one of the beautiful bird cries that Doughty loved and records in *Arabia Deserta*. Doughty carries the bird metaphor through to the narrator's overt moral comment, which portrays our relation to truth as that of a young bird to its mother. Without its deft use of dissonance, this passage would be much less effectively ironic.

E   *Register 5: Direct*

Sâlem said, rising, "Leave one of them!" This last shot he reserved for me; and I felt it miserable to die here by their barbarous hands without defence. "Fheyd, he said again, is all sure?—and one remains?" (II, 497)

We find no overly melodious or harsh sounds here, and no use of Arabic words or particularly Arabic rhythms. Salem's utterance uses direct, abrupt music to create suspense and threat. His monosyllabic remarks convey directly and admirably the threat of shooting that Khalil faces, and even the periodic suspense of "and one remains" is very abbreviated. Similarly, the narrator's grant of a glimpse into Khalil's thoughts is very straightforward (despite the slight ironic distance of "reserved" and the passive construction "I felt it miserable," which indicates Khalil's impotence) and does not rely on musical expression to make or underline its point. In the Salem-Fheyd incident, there are examples of a more heightened and musical style, but in this passage all is subordinated to spare, direct action.

F   *Register 6: Plain*

The Fukara women alighted an hour before noon, in the march, to milk their few ewes and goats. Every family and kindred are seen wayfaring by themselves with their cattle. (I, 220–21)

This anthropological description of the Beduins' herding customs does not employ sound to make its point. We are kept on the surface of the facts by the simple and direct expression of the narrator which comes close to that of normal contemporary English. But the placement of the phrase "in the march" in the middle, rather than at the beginning or end of the first sentence, and the use of "in" rather than "on" or "during" in the phrase, remind us that Doughty in *Arabia Deserta* is never really "plain." In the use of the words "kindred" and "wayfaring" in the second sentence we even catch a very faint biblical echo.

Even in this most "plain" of registers, we see how Doughty's style in the entire book *is* content. He took biblical associations and the Arabic syntax and diction that reminded him of the Bible, and made his style incorporate these things. From his own personality, he took an essential sobriety, dignity, detached irony, reliability, and belief in older English, and worked these into his very sentences by using a consistent set of devices and rhythms (which, however, he varies in amount) over twelve hundred pages. No style is so directly an outgrowth of its content and its author's unique personality, and no style in English captures the atmosphere of Semitic culture as seen by an Englishman so well as *Arabia Deserta*'s. Literally no one but Doughty could have written these sentences, which express his vision of the East (and West) so convincingly, and carry us along with him hypnotically, especially in the most melodious passages.

The close formal study of the book leaves us with its author, Doughty himself, as its ultimate "explanation." He has created a unique work as the mirror of his own mind. Although composed of known elements, and influenced by the same forces molding others in his age, the very large sum of originality that remains after the familiar elements have been subtracted is the mark of his genius.

CHAPTER 3

Travels in Arabia Deserta: *Themes*

I *The Problem*

WHY did Charles Doughty deliberately ignore the warnings of his friends and enter Arabia calling himself a Christian instead of accepting an expedient Islamic disguise, and continue traveling there for nearly two long years in the face of opthalmia, bilharzia, xenophobic intolerance, and an almost total lack of funds? This remains the fundamental problem at the core of *Arabia Deserta* and it has not been solved. Since Doughty apparently did not understand his own deepest reasons for this voyage of geographical and self-discovery, a permanent romantic aura of endless striving for a mysterious and perhaps unattainable goal continues to surround the book and its main character, Khalil.

Scholars have taken Doughty's vague statements of purpose, which appear in the prefaces to the second and third editions of his masterpiece, as mere starting points rather than conclusions for their own research into his character. In the second preface Doughty writes:

> Of surpassing interest to those many minds, which seek after philosophic knowledge and instruction, is the Story of the Earth, Her manifold living creatures, the human generations and Her ancient rocks.
> Briefly, and with such views as these, not worldly aims, a disciple of the divine Muse of Spenser and Venerable Chaucer ... I wandered on.... (ix)

In the third he adds an additional reason for his journey: " ... we almost feel ourselves carried back to the days of the nomad Hebrew Patriarchs. ... And we are the better able to read the bulk of the Old Testament books ..." (xvi).

These stated reasons place Doughty in the nineteenth-century tradition of Arabian exploration delineated by Peter Brent:

It was now . . . that a new passion for archeology, combined with a conviction that the literal truth of the Bible might yet be proved, brought busy travellers . . . in search of the evidence craved by the west. Men risked reputations and even lives in the effort to copy . . . the ancient inscriptions that would, they hoped, clarify once and for all the early history, not merely of Arabia, but of the whole human race.[1]

This may explain why Doughty started his trip to Medain Salih to "squeeze" Nabataean inscriptions, but not why he insisted on being called a *Nasrâny* and plunging into Arabia in spite of all the very good reasons for not doing so.

A strange reticence about Khalil's motives characterizes the narrator of *Arabia Deserta*. Even the very minimal statement from the second preface, quoted above, had to be wrung out of Doughty by a cagey letter from T. E. Lawrence, who was no less fascinated by the question of Doughty's motivation than all who have followed him have been:

My hopes were that perhaps you would just put down on paper, easily, the "why" you went to Arabia. I don't mean Medain Salih, but to write something: and it would be exceedingly interesting if you would say how you wrote it—the relation between the notes you took and the finished book: and how you were able to take such notes without being stopped.[2]

The only information Lawrence ever received in reply to this boldly casual query is the second preface, including an unsatisfactory note that "I wrote as I could," which in no way describes the complex relationship between the notebooks and the finished product, as we have seen. When he burned the manuscript of *Arabia Deserta*, Doughty demonstrated the same reticence about his literary art that marks the question of motivation.

Two years of suffering in a hostile climate seem to demand stronger reasons than a desire to explore a monotonous terrain, recreate the biblical experience, and contribute to the language of Spenser and Chaucer. A down-to-earth explanation of the long stay would be that Doughty was imprisoned at Kheybar, delayed by Horeysh's nonchalance at an important moment, and kept waiting by delays in the *kella* and at Aneyza, as well as by his illnesses and chronic lack of means. But these are only circumstantial delays and do not explain the narrator's and Khalil's praise of the Beduin way of life as the best in the world (II, 240, 245, 300), Khalil's statement that he might be wander-

ing in Arabia for "'ten years'" (I, 444), and his insistence on living with
the Beduin and then visiting Kheybar despite all difficulties; or his continued courting of trouble by refusing to countenance Islam even for
a moment.

Near the end of the book, when Khalil has miraculously reached
safety at et-Tayif, the narrator mentions the Rub al Khali, or mysterious Empty Quarter of Arabia, and remarks: "Now my health failed
me; and otherwise I had sought to unriddle that enigma" (II, 524). So
if Khalil had not been sick, he would have continued indefinitely
searching out the sands of Arabia! And when he did reluctantly leave,
Doughty went to India, not to England, interested in further Eastern
experience. As Lawrence and others have known, Doughty's motivation goes beyond superficial interest in inscriptions and forced circumstances deep into his mind and character.

As an artist, Doughty understood very well the romantic value of
leaving his motivation obscure. This is why he begins the book with a
complex, retrospective ninety-word sentence that raises the question of
his motives for the journey and leaves it hanging: "'. . . what moved
thee, or how couldst thou take such journeys into the fanatic Arabia?'"
(I, 1). By placing this question at the beginning of the book, Doughty
starts the reader on a search for the answer that parallels Khalil's own
voyage of discovery. The challenge to the reader is something like this:
"I don't know why I went, but maybe you can discover the reason
somewhere in my book." The close reader who has entered Doughty's
special world will not come away from the quest empty-handed. For
in the book as a whole Doughty the artist has implied six reasons for
Khalil's drive into Arabia; followed like strands through *Arabia
Deserta,* these six reasons become its major themes. They are what
Arabia Deserta is "about," and supply its continued interest down to
our day.

II   *The St. John Theme*

Doughty went into Arabia because *he wanted to return to the pure
sources of language—for him, the Semitic oral tradition which was
written down in the Old Testament. In doing so, he would put himself—and, through his book, the reader—in closer touch with God.*
This is the story of Khalil's search for ancient inscriptions, and biblical
parallels in the Arabic language of the Beduin, and Doughty the artist's
use of the results of that search to make *Arabia Deserta* itself. As artist,

Doughty wanted to capture the biblical manner of speech, not merely by recalling English translations, but by approximating Arabic—which resembles Hebrew—in his own English style. He wanted to give the reader insight into the style of the Bible and revivify the English language by making him *feel* biblical style and customs as closely as possible, as he tells us directly in the third preface. He wants us to hear the Arabs speak so we may know how the Hebrews spoke and strive to speak a more forceful English ourselves, like him "resisting . . . the decadence of the English language"[3] as he wrote to his biographer. For Doughty, as for the Beduin, words and God are inevitably connected, and by purifying English usage Doughty would be purifying prayer and thought, man's channels to God. We may title this the St. John theme, for Doughty's concern for the Word and its religious connotations reminds us of John 1: "In the beginning was the Word, and the Word was with God, and the Word was God."

Khalil demonstrates an interest in copying inscriptions from rocks, but he is shown to be at least equally interested in the observation of Arabic, particularly Beduin, speech. The eight pages devoted to the details of Beduin oral customs and art (I, 262–70) as well as comments interspersed throughout the book, confirm our view of Khalil as a man who obsessively sought out and observed closely these customs (in spite of the narrator's apology on I, 268 for Khalil's not having observed them closely enough!), and our view of Doughty the artist as a man deeply influenced by these observations in his own writing.

On I, 127 the narrator tells us openly of Khalil's lack of proficiency in Arabic through the mouth of Mohammed Aly, but also of his preference for Beduin speech:

The aga unlettered but erudite in the mother tongue distinguished to us three kinds of the Arabic utterance: *el-aly*, the lofty style as when a man should discourse with great personages; *el-wast*, the mean speech, namely for the daily business of human lives; and that all broken, limping and threadbare, *ed-dûn*, the lowly,—"and wellah as this speaking of Khalîl." Nevertheless that easy speech, which is born in the mouth of the Beduins, is far above all the school-taught language of the town.

Just what Khalil liked in the form and content of "the cheerful musing Beduin talk, a lesson in the travellers' school of mere humanity" (I, 262), we see in the following narrator's memories and comments: (1) "*the Beduwy's mind is in his eyes*'" (I, 256) and "The nomad's eyes are fixed upon the crude congruity of Nature" (I, 263); (2) "All their speech is homely; they tell of bygone forays and of adventures in their desert lives" (I, 263); (3) "The nomad's fantasy is high, and that is ever clothed in religion. . . . Wonder, as all their Semitic life, has the voice of religion" (I, 264). As narrator, Doughty clarifies the third point and reveals its impact on him by spontaneously recalling many phrases used by the Beduin: "A few turns and ornaments of their speech, come suddenly to my remembrance. . . . 'Nay, the Lord give thee peace;' . . . 'The Lord lead thee;' . . . 'The Lord show mercy to thy deceased parentage'" (I, 264). The Beduin even compare favorably to Christians in their religious use of language: "Semites, it is impossible that they should ever blaspheme, in manner of those of our blood, against the Heavenly Providence" (I, 265). (4) The narrator notes with approval the ubiquitous Beduin oral poet, or "kassâd" (I, 263), who employs a special poetic language, divorced from mundane life, which a participatory audience echoes. Doughty's attraction to the ancient sensory concreteness and oral epic-heroic quality closely allied to religious feeling, of Beduin language, appears in his own poetry of Cuan's bardic Christian hymns in Dawn in Britain and in Adam Cast Forth's tactile view of the world. Arabia Deserta, however, recaptures the Beduin linguistic atmosphere far more effectively than the poetry because of its original prosaic weave of Arabic elements, biblical parallelism and allusion, and older English speech forms.

What Khalil did not like about Beduin speech—as the narrator tells us—is its "jesting ribaldry" (I, 265), which must have reminded him of Chaucer, who is criticized for the same quality in Mansoul; "raging of the tongue" (I, 266) or intemperate cursing; and "impudent promises and petulant importunity" (I, 265), or its whining and wheedling quality. Further, although Beduin oaths saved Khalil's life three times (once in Hayil, twice when he was forsaken in the desert) by obliging those who heard them to protect him, these oaths were not as binding as Khalil's own Englishman's "word," as the narrator tells us: "my word was accepted without an oath in Arabia" (I, 176). Even the negative qualities of Beduin speech, however, remind the narrator of the Bible, because he uses the examples of Kings Ahab and Saul, and David and Jonathan, and the prophet Ezekiel to illustrate speech patterns found among the Beduin.

T. E. Lawrence states that the Arabs he questioned remembered Khalil as a silent man. This is partially because he was listening so intently. And the author of Arabia Deserta has filled it with dialogue which is so new to our ears (and so accurately rendered) that it forces us to *listen* just as Khalil did: "'Eigh! here comes Khalîl: *márhabba,* welcome, O Khalîl; make place for Khalîl; pass up, Khalîl, and sit thou here beside me'" (I, 231); "'Well, but the war with those of your kindred and the Sooltân!—Is he not killing up the Nasâra like sheep flocks? so God give him the victory!—say this, Khalîl, *Ullah yunsur es-Sooltân*'" (I, 274).

In his very first sentence in the book, Doughty the artist deliberately emphasizes the spoken word: "new voice" is placed first and isolated from "old friend" to set it off; we have the phrase "which is *called* Straight" (my italics); the "'Tell me'" is strongly stressed and heard before we know who is asking it; and a long spoken question-arabesque powerfully concludes the last half of the whole sentence. Even "Ullah" and "God" are both used in this sentence to describe God in order to awaken our consciousness of the difference sound makes. And throughout the book, Doughty uses every poetic technique possible to awaken our hearing, as we have seen in our discussion of assonance, alliteration, and other features of his style.

For Doughty the artist and Khalil the seeker of spoken and written words, language, far from the contemptible and inadequate tool that many recent detractors have held it to be, actually constitutes the means by which we go back into our origins and thereby forward into a renewed, purified, and more concrete contact with our God. The theme of the search for authentic language constitutes the great primary subject of the book, as Doughty's style constantly reminds us. Doughty's special grammar, including its attempt to recapture the rhythm of Arabic dialogue, serves to awaken, cleanse, and reorient our slumbering aural faculty.

III   *The Adam Cast Forth Theme*

Doughty went into Arabia because *he wanted to experience the Adamic isolation, direct contact with God, and penance.* In short, suffering cleanses. As in the cases of T. E. Lawrence and Wilfred Thesiger after him, Arabia discovered in Doughty a masochistic streak that had been only latent before. Hogarth's orthodox biography never takes us below the surface of the man to tell us this, but Khalil's actions and statements in *Arabia Deserta* reveal it clearly enough: instead of turning back time and again when he could have (I, 204–5, 279, 409), he insists on forcing himself deeper and deeper into Wahabi country, pro-

claiming himself a Christian all the way. The "'Sâiehh'" (I, 272) or
"world's wanderer," as Khalil terms himself, learns through suffering
and isolation. As the narrator writes of the Beduin, "They see but the
indigence of the open soil about, full of dangers, and hardly sustaining
them, and the firmament above them, habitation of the Divine Salvation" (I, 264). In this quotation, the narrator refers to the purifying
feeling of direct, harsh contact with nature and man that Khalil no less
than the Beduin experiences in the desert.

This theme of spiritual cleansing through suffering is present, as are
all others, in the very first sentence of the book. The voice that abruptly
hails Khalil and his friend's reference to the "garden of God" remind
us of God's voice as it calls to Adam in Gen. 3: "And the LORD God
called unto Adam, and said unto him, Where art thou?" In the first
sentence, the narrator places Khalil in the position of Adam after the
Fall and expulsion from Eden. Damascus appears as Eden before the
Fall, complete with "new blossoming orchards," the fertility of spring,
companionship, and "the peace and assurance of Ullah." Before his
journey, Khalil walked in these gardens of Damascus as unfallen man.
But the "fanatic Arabia" has been the world after the eating of the
apple, the place of harsh, lonely trials and the absence of a benevolent
God. When we meet Khalil at the beginning of *Arabia Deserta* in this
sentence, he has already cast himself out of Eden and has returned to
it only briefly.

When we meet him in the opening sentence then, Khalil as fallen
Adam sees all men in and out of Eden as crooked rather than
Straight—*including his closest friends and even himself*, and the
friend who holds his hand in this sentence as well. All those he has met
on his journey have their faults, like Chaucerian pilgrims, as the narrator tells us and as we see through the dialogues of the various characters. A series of Beduin guides betray him in the most desperate circumstances. Mohammed en Nejumy, Khalil's only friend and protector
at Kheybar, "though so worthy a man and amiable, was a soldier in his
own household. . . . Once I saw him . . . rise to strike his son!" (II, 141).
And "I found the good man as weak as water in the end of these evils:
he had I know not what secret understanding now with the enemy
Abdullah, and, contrary to his former words, he was unwilling that I
should receive my things until my departure!" (II, 202).

Abdullah el Kenneyny fills Mohammed's office of friend and protector at Aneyza, but when Khalil is sick "there came no friends to visit
me. Arabs are always thus—almost without the motions of a generous

nature" (II, 397). El Kenneyny double checks the figures of the bank
draft Khalil requests him to cash, and even though the narrator tells us
that Abdullah did this to instruct Khalil, he significantly reports Abdullah's words "'Trust not Khalîl, to any man! not even to me'" (II, 418).
When Khalil must hide in an orchard two and half miles outside
Aneyza, "there came none of my acquaintance to visit the Nasrâny.
Their friendship is like the voice of a bird upon the spray: if a rumour
frighten her she will return no more" (II, 441), in the words of the
retrospective narrator. And, instead of meeting appreciation and
understanding, Khalil's honest talk gets him into continual trouble, as
it might in any society. This policy of frankness might have been
"'wise folly'" (II, 343) as Khalil puts it, since no one could claim that
he was a disguised spy, but the reactions it produced could not raise
his estimation of mankind.

In view of the untrustworthiness of the humanity all around him,
we are not surprised when Khalil himself, despite his moral stamina
and high sense of personal worth as *Nasrâny*, Englishman, and individual, begins to feel somehow stained, guilty, and like an outlaw himself. As a Puritan, Khalil has an ingrown sense of original sin and guilt
in any case, following Adam's eating of the apple. Arabia simply
developed this feeling in him: after more than a year of hardship and
blame, it would be strange if this were not the case, especially in view
of his chosen self-identification with the role of Christian wanderer.

Toward the end of the book, in the Aneyza section, the narrator
mentions the corrupting influence of Khalil's ostracism on his self-
esteem (and Khalil's learning from the experience) more than once:
"Cold is the outlaw's life; and I marked with a natural constraint of
heart an alienation of the street faces, a daily standing off of the faint-
hearted, and of certain my seeming friends" (II, 369); "And seeing the
daily darkening and averting of the Wahâby faces, I had a careful
outlaw's heart under my bare shirt; though to none of them had I done
anything but good,—and this only for the name of the young prophet
of Galilee and the Christian tradition!" (II, 395). After an attack by
rock-throwing children, Khalil's rejection by society (and his sense of
worthlessness and Kafkaesque guilt) reaches a pitch, as the narrator
informs us:

I returned through the bazaar with the *deyik es-súdr* [heartsickness]—for
what heart is not straitened, being made an outlaw of the humanity about
him? were it even of the lowest savages! . . . Then Sheykh Nâsir came sternly

stalking by me, without regard or salutation!—but welcome all the experience of human life. The sun was set, and the streets were empty, when I came again to the door of my desolate house; where weary and fasting, in this trouble, I lay down and slept immediately. (II, 403)

Notable in these passages are the narrator's religious association of the outlaw's heart and the "bare shirt" of suffering which he had called essential to Arabian travels (I, 56), his use of the word "straitened" which reminds us of the "Straight" street of Damascus which Khalil paces in the first sentence of the book, and the comment "welcome all the experience of human life." Khalil is so exhausted by his role as weary, fasting, outlawed Adam that he can only fall into a neurotically immediate sleep to escape his trials, but the retrospective narrator subtly ties all the suffering to a refinement of the spirit by mentioning the "bare shirt" and "fasting" and the religious lesson to be learned by the experience of suffering: the "Straight" road of Puritan suffering confines but liberates by teaching.

However little he likes it, Khalil comes to accept his role as Adam suffering for the sins of all mankind—his own harsh frankness, dogmatism, and intolerance included—and to learn from it. By calling himself a *Nasrâny*, he has willingly though painfully submitted himself to these hardships as a puritanical cleansing process, to expiate the sense of original sin in his soul. He has deliberately cast himself out of the Eden of Damascus in a long journey into hell, overcoming rough trials that he could never have found in the smoother Syria or Europe. He has purified himself in preparation for assuming a new identity (the St. Paul theme, following) by rubbing himself up against the jarring reality bespoken in the short *a* sounds of "fanatic" Arabia of the first sentence in the book. Suffering makes the "bare shirt" and "clean human heart" (I, 56) of the traveler even barer and cleaner.

IV   *The St. Paul Theme*

Doughty went into Arabia *to explore his ideals and find a new identity*. This is the St. Paul theme, and constitutes the completing half of the Adam Cast Forth role of Khalil—here Doughty stresses not his sufferings, but the new creed and new identity he evolved as a result of them, when he grew into the name and role of Khalil, friend of God, just as Paul accepted a new role and identity by changing *his* name. Somewhere on the road back to Damascus, Doughty has shed his old identity like Paul and become not just the disguised *hakîm* or doctor of the body who set out, but the healer of the soul or traditionally Christian "Good Physician," who preaches to the Arabs by word and example a peculiar Christian morality and set of standards. This new morality of Khalil's would be difficult for people in any culture to obey, since it demands that they defy their own people and self-interest to help a stranger who continually stresses his strangeness and utter help-lessness and the wrongness of their way of life. As Stanley Fish comments on the role of the "Good Physician," "he tells his patients what they *don't* want to hear in the hope that by forcing them to see them-selves clearly, they may be moved to change the selves they see."[4] We begin to feel while reading *Arabia Deserta* that Khalil has subcon-sciously decided from the start—by choosing to call himself a *Nas-rány*—to test the Christian ideal of humility, turning the other cheek, poverty, and asceticism by trying it out against a totally hostile envi-ronment, to see if it will really work, and if he is worthy of it, and we watch him grow into the role of exemplar and preacher of this doctrine.

As Khalil leaves Damascus to join the pilgrimage caravan at the start of his journey, the narrator makes explicit his identification with St. Paul: "As we turned from the long city street, that which in Paul's days was called 'The Straight' . . . some of the bystanders . . . setting upon me their eyes, said to each other, 'Who is this? Eigh!'" (I, 4–5). As a further foreshadowing of his later spiritual development, Khalil tries already during the pilgrimage to stop a beating "as humanity required" (I, 14), thus expanding his role of doctor to include the soul, despite the riskiness of this move for him. Next, we witness him taking Mohammed Aly's blow in the face without striking back. Then he refuses to consider killing, even in self-defense, when his guides turn treacherous, as the narrator tells us: "in this faintness of body and spirit I could not tell; I thought that a man should forsake life rather than justice, and pollute his soul with outrage." We hear his simple question "'what need of violence?'" to Sheikh Aly who unjustly expels him from Aneyza. And we finally see his climactic handing of his pistol, butt first, to the half-mad Fheyd, as if daring him to use it, when he might simply have shot Fheyd first, justifiably. And there are many, many more such occasions when Khalil chooses to place himself in the passive role and take what comes, even beyond the demands of expediency, as Jonathan Bishop has pointed out.[5]

In addition to this amazing turning of the other cheek and courting

of suffering by calling himself a Christian, we see in Khalil the further
Christian elements of an attraction to poor people ("I blessed him and
said it was the best of all nourishment," II, 67), desire to have few
belongings ("rejoicing inwardly, that I might now bear all I possessed
in the world," II, 334), praise of a frugal diet ("I praised the simple
diet of Arabia," II, 514), ideal of universal love ("'Every creature is
rasûl Ullah!'" II, 380), and, as we shall see, preaching. We are not
surprised when we meet Khalil, after his journey, back on Paul's
Straight Street in Damascus, in the retrospective first sentence of *Arabia Deserta*. Because he like Paul developed a new religion out of his
experiences in the desert, the friend's voice of this sentence is "new":
Khalil is a new man who hears old voices differently than he had
before his trip.

The retrospective narrator's defense of Khalil's doctrine of passive
resistance and asceticism appears in a remarkable and much-quoted
passage, which serves as a summary list of the component spiritual
qualities that Khalil developed during his travels:

The traveller must be himself, in men's eyes, a man worthy to live under the
bent of God's heaven, and were it without a religion: he is such who has a
clean human heart and long-suffering under his bare shirt; it is enough, and
though the way be full of harms, he may travel to the ends of the world. Here
is a dead land, whence, if he die not, he shall bring home nothing but a perpetual weariness in his bones. (I, 56)

The religious language of this passage underlines the narrator's claim
that Arabia actually *demands* saintliness and martyrdom of a traveler.
He will suffer and gain nothing at all, and must not travel as a mere
tourist on the pilgrim road. In fact, this is Khalil's own ideal; other
travelers, notably the swashbuckling Burton, had no intention of
becoming saints or martyrs in Arabia and therefore disguised their
Christianity.

The narrator's defense of the religion of suffering and passive resistance which Khalil evolved in Arabia goes beyond simple statement to
become a kind of preaching to the reader, in which Khalil is used as
an idealized exemplar despite his occasional faults of loss of temper
and harshness. The narrator admonishes us just as Khalil admonishes
rather than simply speaks to the Arabs whom he meets. When Swoysh
of a rival tribe asks Khalil half-jokingly to poison the wells of the How-
eitat, Khalil sententiously replies: "'My religion bids us to deal with all
men as brethren; your silver, above ground and under it, cannot move

me"'" (I, 404). Recounting Khalil's departure from Hayil after many torments, the narrator sums up by stating that

The Arabs are to be won by gentleness and good faith, they yield to just arguments, and before I left Hâyil the most of my old foes wished me well in their hearts. To use an unflattering plainness of speech was also agreeable to the part of sûwahh, or wandering anchorite in the fable of human life. (II, 44)

The narrator, with Doughty the artist behind him, tells us how to live no less than Khalil tells the Arabs the same thing. As Khalil's role is that of wandering "anchorite" who must speak the truth to men, forgiving his enemies as he goes, so the narrator presents human life religiously as a "fable."

In answer to his friend Abdullah el Kenneyny's wonder at his anchoritic outspokenness at Aneyza, Khalil states a brief sermon: "'I am this second year, in a perilous country, and have no scathe. Thou hast heard the proverb "Truth may walk through the world unarmed"'" (II, 342). Khalil's statements and way of behavior pass beyond expediency and have become a definite religion. Taken together, this passage and many others like it mean: truth, humility, and turning the other cheek will carry the world before them. Of such beliefs are great religious leaders—and great fanatics—made.

By the end of the book Khalil has become a saint, and the narrator portrays him as such, especially in the climactic Salem-Fheyd incident outside Tayif. We see this incident in religious terms as we witness Khalil's preaching of the good doctrine as his only protection against harm, his withstanding of the temptation to do violence, and the victorious outcome of this trial with the devil, or a Salem who very much resembles the devil. On I, 446, the narrator has told us that the Beduin criticized the Christian doctrine of accepting harm without retaliation: "but it seemed strange to them, that a man must love his adversary in this malicious world, and indeed not just." When Khalil faces Salem, a half-mad outlaw who does not even accept the normal desert rules of hospitality and protection of strangers, he practices and tests the Christian doctrine the Beduin cannot understand, and finds that it works.

To Salem's taunt, "'thou art not afraid!'" Khalil answers with the moral statement, "'Is not Ullah in every place?'" To Salem's threatening "'Dreadest thou not to die,'" he answers again religiously, "'I have not so lived, Moslêm, that I must fear to die'" (II, 502). Khalil's

refusal to show fear is a form of psychological expediency that helped
save his life; but the tone of his defense in these sentences and throughout is specifically Christian. Khalil, like Christ, overcomes the temptation to lose his temper and kill (as he could have easily instead of
handing over his pistol), and decides to trust even the humanity of the
madman Salem as his religion bids him. Salem is characterized by the
narrator, appropriately, as "the tormentor" (II, 495) or the devil; and
he fails to move Khalil to fear or violence.

As Khalil walks over the burning sand, falling on his knees to spare
himself the hot pain in his bare feet during this spiritual test against
Salem, we see him as a saint at the end of a difficult ordeal: " . . . the
sand was as burning coals under my bare feet, so that after every few
steps I must fall on my knees to taste a moment's relief" (II, 499).
Khalil's religious ideal of Christian love wins out over Salem's inhu-
manity and intolerance after almost killing Khalil with its demands of
self-control.

Arrived finally at et-Tayif and safety, Khalil appears even more
strongly as a martyr after an ordeal, owing to the narrator's description:

The tunic was rent on my back, my mantle was old and torn; the hair was
grown down under my kerchief to the shoulders, and the beard fallen and
unkempt; I had bloodshot eyes, half blinded, and the scorched skin was
cracked to the quick upon my face. . . . Whilst the barber was doing, the
stalwart Turkish official anointed my face with cooling ointments; and his
hands were gentle as a woman's,—but I saw no breakfast in that hospice!
After this he clad me, my weariness and faintness being such, like a block, in
white cotton military attire; and set on my head a fez cap. (II, 506)

The specifically religious language of this passage ("anointed," "hospice") and its symbolism of austere white clothing and fez form an
unforgettable image of Khalil as pure secular priest who has survived
all the trials imposed by an ostensibly jealous and harsh but actually
benevolent God to prove that Christian love is stronger than hate.
Khalil has become an instrument of this God like an ancient prophet,
or like Paul, and Doughty the artist tells us through Khalil's example
and the narrator's overt statements in his testament, *Arabia Deserta*,
how to live.

Not everyone has liked Khalil's neo-Christian religion of humanity,
but it has been noticed as an essential strand in the book. Thus Richard
Burton notices unfavorably this masochistic, saintlike belief, enumer-

ates in his review of the book all the indignities it chronicles, and concludes: "I cannot, for the life of me, see how the honoured name of England can gain aught by the travel of an Englishman who at all times and in all places is compelled to stand the buffet from knaves that smell of sweat."[6] Stronger or more aggressive natures rebel at the idea of self-abasement as a defense; and the Beduin criticism (also echoed by some Jewish thinkers) of the Christian ideal of loving enemies has some force. But Doughty has unforgettably depicted the for him total triumph of this way of life through his character Khalil. In the Adam Cast Forth theme, we saw Khalil accepting the role of guilty human and allowing punishment to cleanse him instead of rebelling against it, just like the fallen Adam in his poem of that name. As St. Paul–Khalil he transforms this suffering into a positive ideal of Christian humility which withstands all external and internal spiritual assaults to preach one powerful point: Christianity works.

V   *The Other Culture Theme*

The high tension of Khalil's contact with Islam throughout the book indicates a "culture shock"—a repulsion from and attraction to another culture—as we have learned to call this phenomenon. Doughty went into Arabia *to define himself against the other culture*. Doughty knew about Islam and Arabs before he ever set foot in Arabia. As Mrs. Robbins commented to me in conversation, we can detect in the early European–North African diary a certain special interest in the Arabs on Doughty's part even at this early date of his life. The following passage from the diary typescript, now in the Gonville and Caius Library, foreshadows the interest that led to Arabian travels:

Thus I had the happiness to pass the Sunday day of rest and cheerfulness in some hospitality and quiet. The Arabs and our host joined their hands and kissed each with a sort of fervour at their meeting much in the Italian manner who have it perhaps from the arabs. There I lay in security and put away my pistol.
the tents are of sackcloth of hair of ruddy and black stripes and suspended upon sticks. (20)

These remarks, written when Doughty was traveling with a "caravan of 10 men with mules and asses loaden with dates" going from "Biskra to Bon Saida" (19) in 1872, are notable for their incipient fascination,

the reference to Sunday's special qualities (echoed by the narrator in
Arabia Deserta, I, 83), the pistol (again to appear in *Arabia Deserta*),
and their plain language in contrast to the developed style of Doughty's
masterpiece. In addition to this preparation for Arabia, he spent a year
in Damascus studying Arabic just prior to his travels, and heard warnings about Arabian dangers. So he knew about the other culture and
the risks he would run, but was obsessed with pitting himself against
the strange, alien society that he had just begun to fathom.

In the very first sentence in the book, we see the implied struggle
delineated, with both its attraction to and stronger repulsion from
Islamic culture that marks Doughty's whole book. In this sentence, the
use of "Ullah" and "God" demonstrates not only the joint basis of
Christian and Moslem belief, but differences as well. "Ullah" sounds
strange to an English-speaking person's ear. The mention of Damascus
with its strange street, the friend's willingness to take Khalil by the
hand (an impossible show of male intimacy in a puritanical society),
and the circumlocutions of the friend's speech, all indicate that we are
in a world very different from our own. In the narrator's portrayal, this
new world takes on the colors of the famous "mysterious East"—
despite his denials of "Orientalism" (I, 56), or false picturesqueness—
replete with strange names, strange customs, strange syntax. While
Doughty strove to report facts and feelings accurately, his semi-Arabic
style and Chaucerian vision cast a romantic veil over every part of the
book, as we have seen. We move in the realm of the "fanatic Arabia,"
a term chosen consciously by Doughty for use in this first sentence to
recall centuries of Christian conflict with Islam, and which echoes the
tone of the twelfth-century traveler Saewulf of Worcester, who writes
of "Arabia, hostile to Christians."

Khalil's universalizing, which serves to placate the Arabs in the face
of immediate confrontations and which holds that "'I take every religion to be good, by which men are made better,'" and his long sermon
on universal religion to El Kenneyny ("'Every religion ... is born of
human needs, and her utterance is true religion ... ,'" II, 381) are only
sops for the moment, because the narrator, under no social pressure to
be tolerant, makes it clear that Islam cannot make men good, but
rather the opposite: "The nations of Islam, of a barbarous fox-like
understanding, and persuaded in their religion, that 'knowledge is only
of the koran,' cannot now come upon any way that is good" (I, 101).
And there are many, many more such intolerant passages from the
narrator.

Thomas J. Assad discusses what Doughty consciously disliked—and to a lesser degree, liked—about the Arabs: Doughty's basically anti-Arab attitude, which Assad subtly attributes to a "thwarted inclination to sympathize with the Arabs" and a resentment that they, "living in a land which was sacred to Doughty by virtue of its role in the march of humanity ... ignored the prestige of his beloved country and detested its religion,"[7] predominates in the book. Doughty as Khalil and especially as narrator displays irrational prejudice on very many occasions. Why, for instance. is monogamy inevitably to be preferred to polygamy? The Beduin give an excellent defense of polygamy, namely, that it takes time and experience to find a good partner for life (I, 298), but Khalil remains unmoved, and the narrator's only argument against polygamy seems to rest on a vague kind of puritanical frugality in wives as in money (I, 24), and is not very forceful or persuasive. The narrator repeats the old anti-Jewish slander about greediness as if it were truth (I, 265), but when it happens that the Moslems have a similar prejudice about Christian greed, he immediately rejects it as gross stupidity (I, 387). We see today all too clearly that the narrator remains blind to the prejudices of his own class and society in himself, ascribing to his society always the highest motives of Christianity, while he takes every ignorant Moslem's prejudice as indicative of the highest law of Islam. The narrator understands that the practice as opposed to the theory of religion frequently leaves much to be desired, as when he criticizes Syrian Greek Christian behavior and superstition, but he never admits Islam and Judaism to spiritual equality with Christianity, and frequently indulges in vicious saber rattling against these two religions, actually suggesting that Mecca and Medina should be "led captive" (II, 379) by Christians so that "the Moslemîn should become as Jews," that is, powerless and oppressed.

Two opinions, one contemporary and Norman Douglas's more modern view, help put the narrator's (and Khalil's) prejudices in a balanced perspective. The contemporary reviewer for the science journal *Nature* wrote about Doughty that:

He is a man, by his own confession, of blunt and plain speech, improvident and forgetful, with an old world belief in the falsity of Mohammedanism and the Koran, and the iniquity of countenancing them even by a politic word. His explorations took place at the time of the war between Turkey and Russia, when the fanaticism of the Mohammedans of Arabia was excited to the utmost, and he had to leave Damascus at the outset of his journey without any letters of help from the British Consul.[8]

If Doughty was upset by his reception in Arabia during the Russo-Turkish War, perceived by the Arabs as an Islamic-Christian conflict, he should only have asked himself (before blaming Islam) how a Beduin, speaking broken English and without a passport or much money, would have fared wandering around England during a war between England and some Islamic country in the 1870s. No doubt he would have been interned in a prison camp as a dangerous spy without ado—especially if he had been caught making maps and notes. Indeed, in a letter to an unnamed correspondent (21 June 1879), Doughty reveals the kind of treatment an Arab could expect from the English during the same period he as Khalil was demanding and expecting hospitality from the Arabs:

The like treatment I found from the Anglo-Indians at Aden because arrived from Arabia I was clad as an Arab, and the little cockney adjutant in the camp insulted me before his British troop and the Commanding officer would not permit me to visit Perim. . . . In sum they had taken me in their imagination for a Russian spy.[9]

But when Khalil is asked in *Arabia Deserta* by Amm Mohammed how he would fare in Khalil's country, Khalil's reply is always favorable (II, 158–59)! As the narrator of *Arabia Deserta*—who does not realize the implications for himself of his own statement—puts it, "Patriotism and Religion! In the one and the other there seem to us to be sweetly comprehended all virtues; and yet in the excess they are springs from which flow out extreme mischiefs!" (I, 549).

Norman Douglas, writing of his re-reading of the book after World War I, makes an important point by recording his own changed reactions to it:

Moving once more among those sinewy articulations . . . I become aware of a change. . . . Whatever the cause, I now go through these pages with a more hearty sympathy for the Beduins—that "merry crew of squalid wretches, iniquitous, fallacious, fanatical"—and feeling of resentment . . . against our Occidental institutions; a distrust of those white people who can make such an exhibition of ourselves as they have done of late.[10]

Doughty did not change his views of British and Western superiority even after World War I, as *Mansoul* testifies; but this is the difference between his Victorian perception of the world which he as Khalil and narrator gives us in his book, and our perception of it, which—especially after World War II—is more sympathetic to other cultures and more cognizant of our own failures. However, because Doughty the artist has included the Arabs' forceful responses to Khalil's and the narrator's criticisms—such as their attacks on Christianity, colonialism, and monogamy—the book offers a substantially wider point of view on the cultural question than Khalil and the narrator are prepared to allow, as we saw in our discussion of literary personae in the last chapter.

If the narrator despises Islam's polygamy, Mohammed's character, the slave trade, women's status (he would idealize them in the Victorian manner), Wahabi intolerance, Turkish corruption, Arab fatalism, and Beduin unreliability, he expresses openly his pleasure in Beduin freedom of movement and governance, their simplicity of life, biblical customs, individual heroism, and the supposed nobility of the upper class, and even the frugal life of the Arabian town. But far more interesting is the subconscious process of attraction to and imitation of Arabic culture that he unknowingly portrays in Khalil.

Although Khalil never experiences what I have elsewhere termed the drama of "the two veils" of T. E. Lawrence, an absorption into the Arab culture to the point of a weakened English identity, we witness in Khalil an attenuated but nonetheless noticeable process of influence by the other culture. In view of his prejudices, it is almost comic to watch Khalil in his dialogues and in the narrator's description unconsciously begin to imitate some of the "Semitic qualities" that he attributes to the Arabs, including those he despises: a Beduin-like bluntness of opinion, sudden shifts of mind, fatalism, superstition, cursing, even a brief moment of sexual lust under the Puritan exterior.

When asked which way of life is best in the world, Khalil unhesitatingly answers that of "'the houses of hair'" (II, 230), or the Beduin way. He says this after more than a year of Arabian travels, and plainly means that the Beduin way is superior to *all* other possible ways of life, not merely to that of the Arabian town. We are not surprised when people actually think Khalil a Beduin because of his successful adaptation: "These Beduins seeing me broken to the nomad life, enquired; 'were all my people Beduw?'" (II, 307). A mental adaptation complements the physical. Thus, we find the supposedly hard-headed scientific narrator who rejects what he calls Islamic superstition and "irrational" (II, 131) djinn tales admitting that Khalil had "presentiments," or future sight of evil events: "In the same moment a singular presentiment, almost a persuasion, possessed my soul, that the goodly young

man's death was near at hand; and notwithstanding my life daily
threatened in a hazardous voyage and this infirm health, that I should
survive him" (II, 40). At other points in the journey, the narrator shows
Khalil adopting the fatalistic view both condemn in the nomads: "I saw
all would be a vain effort in any peril; the stars were contrary for this
voyage . . ." (I, 570). And on I, 610 the narrator admits Khalil's indul-
gence in Arab-style cursing: " . . . and the child was not less amazed,
when with the suddenness of the Arabs I prayed Ullah to curse his
parentage. . . ."

Finally, there is the brief but telling moment of sexual attraction
that appears in *Arabia Deserta* as a further testimony to Khalil's interest in the Beduin. Unlike T. E. Lawrence's book, where homosexuality
is sometimes a lurid interest, Doughty's is thoroughly heterosexual.
Norman Douglas blames Doughty for neglecting homosexuality in
Arab life, but the Beduin are simply not homosexuals and the narrator's
eye is plainly on the women rather than on the men:

. . . a flaw of wind . . . blew out her summer frock from the neck; and besides
the haggu, or girding lace of leathern plait, they have nothing else upon their
bodies. Lithe were the negroid limbs, shining in the heat, and notwithstanding the alloy of African blood, perfectly well shaped, she seemed a statue of
bronze. . . . she marked how the kafir came on riding with a discreet indifference.(I, 375)

The "kafir" or Khalil is "indifferent," but somehow the narrator has
gotten a good peek! We have a cross-racial sexual interest here as a
further impetus to Khalil's normal masculine curiosity.

An interesting comment by T. E. Lawrence in his introduction tells
us more of the East's influence on Doughty both as Khalil and as
narrator:

The desert inhibits considered judgements; its bareness and openness make
its habitants frank. . . . Doughty felt this contagion of truthfulness sharply
(few travel-journals show a greater sensibility to climate and geography than
this), and among the tribes he delivered himself like them. Even in the villages he maintained an untimely and uncompromising bluntness, . . . in practice the Englishman, and especially the Englishman of family, finds the tribes
to his taste more than the villages, and Doughty everywhere is the outspoken
Beduin. . . .
    Very climatic, too, are his sudden changes of tone and judgement. The
desert is a place of passing sensation. . . . Men do not hold their minds in

suspense for days, to arrive at a just and balanced average of thought. . . . Doughty has mirrored this also for us in himself. One paragraph will have a harsh judgement; the next is warm kindness. (xx–xxi)

So Khalil's bluntness and the narrator's shifts of mood reflect the desert. We should note, however, that while Lawrence's *Seven Pillars of Wisdom* also exemplifies this shifting of mood toward and away from the Arabs and his surroundings, Lawrence as narrator almost never explains the reasons for this shift, while Doughty as narrator always does. He understood his position vis-à-vis the Arabs and never slid into Lawrence's deep confusion of cultures.

From the very first sentence of Doughty's book, where "fanatic Arabia" is mentioned, we are in the realm of a repulsion or "abhorrence, of race" (II, 248) but also of the very real attraction to the Arabs that has captivated every British traveler from Palgrave through Thesiger. Because the overt attraction is minimal in Doughty compared to almost all the others, he represents the clash of cultures theme at its sharpest, and his self-definition against the other culture is the clearest recorded. If the Arabs respected Khalil, it is because of the sharpness of this difference. We are reminded of Mr. Warburton in Somerset Maugham's "The Outstation," who has an ability to respect and yet rule the Malayans because of his own English class snobbishness and the obvious distance he puts between himself and them, while Cooper, the resentful class-hating democrat, is a total failure with his subjects and is finally murdered by them. In the desert, up against another culture, Doughty learned to define himself as English and *Nasrâny* as never before despite (or perhaps because of) his Arabic name, Khalil. And yet Khalil joins hands with his Islamic friends and opponents in a drama both subtle and amusing, and Doughty the artist has worked Arabic into his very sentences and Arabian mood-shifts into his book's structure. In this love-hate, Doughty represents an extreme example of British relations with the Arabs.

VI   *Mapping the Unknowns of Space and Time*

Doughty went into Arabia in order *to map geological, geographical, and historical unknowns.* This is the scientific theme, stressed by Bevis in his article on Doughty's geology, and by D. G. Hogarth. Not the deepest aspect of the book, it cannot be ignored because it constitutes Doughty's most conscious motivation. He stresses this interest in his second preface, and the index entry "Map of Arabia" is one of the longest and most prideful: "Since the *Itinerarium* was published . . . every chartographer of those parts of Asia has founded upon my labours; which I trust to be such that no time shall overthrow them."

In the first sentence in the book, the narrator mentions places four times, dwelling lovingly on their exotic names. "The Peninsula" and "fanatic Arabia" are geographical terms, but the place they define remains vague and mysterious. In contrast, Damascus and the "long street . . . which is called Straight" are more precise geographical points. Khalil conducted his journey in order to introduce scientific mapping of the chaotic Arabia and to define its human and physical topography precisely, as Damascus itself is defined. He loved the biblical past, but insofar as he uses his modern scientific method to understand it, he represents a Victorian intrusion into previously blank areas, just like the explorers who preceded him in Arabia and those who were opening up Africa at the same time.

The narrator's and Khalil's concern with mapping human customs and physical geography appears at every point in the book, and provides a kind of factual ballast, like the whaling chapters of *Moby Dick*. For Khalil, science is like Marlow's rivets in Conrad's *Heart of Darkness*, sanity in the midst of madness. Even during Khalil's perilous troubles with Salem and Fheyd, he worries about the fate of his aneroid barometer in their "brutish hands" (II, 496), and notes every detail of his surroundings, as the narrator tells us. Although weary and sick, he is pleased to make a detour to Tayif just to see this city. Clearly, Khalil is ready to suffer for scientific as well as spiritual matters, and can be seen as a nineteenth-century saint of science.

Khalil's belief in technology accords with his age. In his conversation with El Kenneyny, he ostensibly prefers it to religion: "'But let us enter the indestructible temple-building of science, wherein is truth'" (II, 381). He proudly reviews for Tollog and later for the Ibn Rashids, the Western world's wonders—the Crystal Palace, the telegraph, the discovery of the New World. Both Hamud and Mohammed very presciently ask about the possible importance of petroleum, and Mohammed combines this question with a wise anticolonialism: "He asked also of petroleum; and of the New Continent, where it lay, whether within 'the Ocean.' He listened coldly to my tale of the finding of the New Land over the great seas, and enquired, 'Were no people dwelling in the country when it was discovered?'" (I, 600). Later, in another interesting foreshadowing of the future, Sheikh Ghraneym asks Khalil "'Might there not be made a railroad through Arabia, passing by Aneyza and reaching to Mecca?'" and Khalil answers approvingly, as the narrator informs us, that "there wanted only an occasion for the enterprise" (II, 519). This is the future Hejaz Railway that T. E. Lawrence, as a post-Victorian semi-believer in technology, was to make his reputation destroying! Like Lawrence in *Seven Pillars of Wisdom*, Khalil speaks to the Beduin of the achievements of Western astronomy; but Khalil stresses the glory of Western science rather than its neurotic striving for total control of nature, which Lawrence emphasizes.

We have seen that Doughty as narrator and as Khalil points up the journey's geographical achievements, which remind him of his Scandinavian glacial research as well (I, 429). But this overt emphasis of narrator and protagonist conflicts to some degree with Doughty's artistic instincts. As artist, he does not scientifically order space in textbook fashion, but instead creates a huge sprawling book which follows closely the meandering and illogical pattern of his real-life journey and juxtaposes scientific observation at random with adventure and meditation. Khalil does not go anywhere in a straight line, and neither does Doughty's book. The reader takes away a vast, mysterious, undefined, and cyclical, rather than linearly progressive, impression. Even the narrator must admit that Khalil failed to get to the Wadi Duasir, Riyadh, Mecca, and the Rub al Khali, and failed to inquire enough about Beduin language (II, 268). A vast mystery remains and seeps through the chinks in Khalil's and the narrator's almost superhuman effort to exclude it by listing all possible scientific details, as even the map, appended to the book, with its considerable remaining blank spaces, seems to testify.

Just as Ishmael will never fully know Moby Dick, the great whale, despite all his cetological science, so Doughty the scientist was not able to compute all the facts necessary for understanding Arabia, and he knows it. His understanding of Arabia will be more a matter of the heart than of the head, and it is better for his book as art that this is so, as it is for *Moby Dick*. The mysterious air conjured by the words "the Peninsula" and "fanatic Arabia" in the first sentence makes the book bigger, giving the reader the sense of an incomplete and perhaps incompletable geographical quest, which was in any case broken off in the middle. Arabia survives Khalil's attempt to know it in Doughty's book because *Arabia Deserta* is great art rather than mere scientific report.

What relates to the space—or geography—in the book also holds true for the time—or historical—sense it finally projects. Doughty as Khalil and narrator indicates a clear interest in mapping—through the search for inscriptions and living biblical customs and the use of Sprenger's archeological book—time as well as space, but here as well the reader feels the quest is not fulfilled in spite of the observational genius displayed by Khalil.

Khalil makes clear his interest in the past time of Arabia by telling Tollog that he came primarily for inscriptions (I, 415). And the letter of the Marquis de Vogüé appended to volume 1 of *Arabia Deserta* and Doughty's French volume of Nabataean inscriptions support Khalil's statement. In addition to biblical and Nabataean research, Khalil is interested in tales of the Jews of Kheybar in the postbiblical period, in the fascinating Himyaritic civilization of Yemen, in Aelius Gallus's ill-fated attempt to tap the Yemenite spice trade for Rome. We see the same quest for and addiction to the past at work in Doughty's writing of *Dawn in Britain, Adam Cast Forth,* and *The Titans,* where he pushes the history of mankind and the earth as far back as he is able. Why is he so addicted?

On page one of *Arabia Deserta,* we read that "The headpiece of this chapter represents a vine and pomegranate ornament, carved in relief upon a block of white marble, still lying in the ruinous wilderness of Moab." When Damascus was an empty tract of desert, other gardens bloomed in what is now waste. Volcanoes once erupted in the desert, as at Vesuvius in Doughty's own time. Civilizations rise and fall owing to human and natural causes. By studying the relics and landscape of the Arabian past, Khalil would come to the cultural roots and fate of civilizations, and perhaps understand the future of his own. More even than this, he wanted to find the principles that made biblical civilization so spiritually vital so he could carry the message back out of the desert and preach it like a prophet to his own, in his opinion, decaying (despite its technology) society. As Khalil, he finds Christianity, "progress," and technology superior to Eastern culture. As narrator, he tells us on more than one occasion that we have nothing to learn from the East. But as artist, Doughty emerges from it all with a very Eastern, Ecclesiastean, fatalistic, cyclical view of civilizations that he passes to the reader above and beyond Khalil's and the narrator's belief in "progress."

Khalil has journeyed into Arabia but finds himself at the beginning of the book, in the first sentence, back where he started from, in

Damascus. The use of the plural "journeys" in this sentence when only a single journey is meant causes a repetitive feeling in the reader. The rhyme of "friend"-"when"-"again"-"again" of this sentence reinforces the repetitive, cyclical expression. "New voice" precedes "old friend" in the first section of the sentence. In the friend's dialogue, "former years" precedes "new blossoming orchards." The reversal again reinforces the cyclical impression, as does the asking of the final question of "why did you do it?" *before* the journey itself is narrated.

Doughty's artistic handling of time in the whole book supports the circular, all-time impression of its content, where many ages are telescoped and mixed together to form a strange blend of modern technological consciousness and a weary Kohelethian past feeling. He purposely scrambles time in the whole book as in this first sentence. The narrator supplies dates only sporadically, and infrequently, without the year indication—even though this is a two-year-long journey spread over three actual years, 1876, 1877, 1878—and without providing any rationale for the times he *does* supply the date. So the reader has difficulty in maintaining a sense of the amount of time that elapses between and during each adventure. The different historical and prehistorical periods are not classified and explained—volcanic, Roman, biblical, Himyaritic, pre- and post-Moslem periods exist in suspension together with the recent and present history of Arabia, including the dynastic rivalry between the Ibn Rashids in Hayil and the Ibn Sauds in Riyadh that constitutes the main fact of Arabian history in the nineteenth century. In short, the time factor in the structure of the book itself is as meandering and vague as that of space, which doubles back on itself as Khalil retraces his steps and goes in circles.

Arabia Deserta presents a detailed record of an imprecise journey into mysterious chaos, whose purpose is to chart and order, but whose deliberately scrambled self-report remains a testimony to chaos and Eastern cyclicism rather than to Western linear order and progress. Khalil has attempted to introduce the order of time and space into blank chaos, but actually comes out with the Kohelethian weariness, the "perpetual weariness in his bones" (I, 56) that the narrator names as *the* essential characteristic of Arabian travels throughout the book, and which quality Doughty the artist passes on most forcibly to the reader. No final problems have been solved despite Khalil's discovery of some watercourses; the "Peninsula" is only very partially known in time and space and its challenge only very partially answered in *Arabia Deserta*. This is why Doughty's Arabia, locked for all time in the

pages of his book, fascinates long after the real country has been totally
mapped and charted.

VII   The Theme of Movement, or Eastern "Western"

Doughty went into Arabia *because he liked to move*. In this one way
only, Khalil reminds us of the Nick Carraway who in Fitzgerald's
Great Gatsby finds rest only in a train moving through the Middle
West or in a car speeding some place or other. He reminds us even
more of an American "Western" cowboy hero who is always on the
move seeking new adventures in a savage land, a good-guy outlaw who
braves "noble savage" Indians (the Beduin) and a corrupt town establishment, pistol at the ready, and who refuses to marry and settle down,
only to disappear as abruptly as he has shown up. This is the adventure
theme, and it accounts for a good deal of the dramatic interest of
Doughty's book.

If we take the first sentence as an example, a microcosm of the work
as a whole, movement is everywhere, even if it is circular: "first
returned," "paced again," "long street," "'thou art here again,'"
"'whilst we walk,'" "'what moved thee,'" "'take such journeys.'" The
narrator delights in the traveler's naming of places visited four times
in this sentence alone. There is no definitive answer to the friend's
question "'what moved thee?'" except perhaps the love of movement
and adventure itself.

From the start, we are invited to see Khalil in terms very similar to
the words from the theme song of the television Western "Paladin":
"A knight without honor in a savage land/Paladin, Paladin, where will
you roam?" As Mohammed Aly says after failing to dissuade Khalil
from continuing into Arabia, "'Khalîl is a man too adventurous; there
may nothing persuade him'" (I, 204).

For nineteenth-century Europeans, Arabia occupied a role compa-
rable to that of the American Wild West, as Israel does today for their
descendants. People bored with the supersophisticated North look to
the East with an inevitable sense of adventure, even now. And Khalil's
story really contains all the elements of a Western romance, with the
twist that it is set in the East. In the narrator's portrait, the Beduin are
like American Indians in a Western: "The nomad's mind is ever in the
ghrazzu [raid]; the knave would win, and by whose loss he recks not,
neither with what improbity: men in that squalid ignorance and
extreme living, become wild men" (I, 259). This wildness is part of

what attracts Khalil to Beduin life. Khalil's internment in Kheybar by the wicked commandant Abdullah reads like a Wild West tale of justice perverted by a bad "Sheriff" (the Arabic "Sherîf" comes to mind as a pun) and a corrupt but intolerant "establishment." His cure of Hamud's son Feysal in Hayil during his semijailing there reminds us of the clichéd scene in a Western film where a white doctor saves a chief's son, a scene repeated in Joseph's cure of a Roman's son in *Dawn in Britain*. The Beduin offer him marriage which he refuses to accept, just as he rejects the offers of conversion or "selling out" to the towns-people who would then set him up in business.

Although Khalil lacks the cowboy hero's aggressiveness, his passivity makes him a kind of spiritual cowboy—an original variation—who shakes up the established order without fear. But he does accept a challenge to duel (I, 460–61) and faces down his opponent. Even without his pistol to defend himself, Khalil appears as a chevalier sans peur et sans reproche as he openly defies false authority. At Kheybar, in the coffee "bar" or saloon, he tells Salih the sheikh to find another seat, refusing to yield his own; and when Abdullah's brutal slave Sirur challenges him, he responds without fear:

"I have wandered in many lands, many years, and with a swine such as thou art, I have not met in any place." The timid Hajâz audience was astonished at my words; the most stared into the fire, and mused in their hearts that the Nasrâny had not said amiss. (II, 117)

He shames Fheyd by handing him his pistol in what must be one of the most original showdowns anywhere, and disconcerts Salem by showing fearlessness in the face of death threats. No less than he challenges unjust man, Khalil faces the dangers of the "hard-set face of nature" (I, 405) and disease without flinching, in approved Western-hero stoic manner.

Almost expectedly, justice is done in the end as it always is in a Western. The Sherif at et-Tayif orders Salem punished and Khalil's goods restored. Finally, even the wicked British consulate which had spurned Khalil in Damascus on the first page, truly turning him into an outlaw, calls him to its "open hospitality" in Jidda in the last sentence of the book. Khalil as spiritual cowboy triumphs over everyone—Beduin, Arab townsman, and British official—and sees justice done! Like all heroes he has undergone the stages of separation (his lone sojourn among the Arabs), initiation (tutelage in the ways of Arab town and desert), confrontation (he faces death and hardship constantly), and return (his reception at Tayif and Jidda), and has redeemed society's view of itself as just by virtue of his stark survival. Khalil's story is actually a wonderful variation on the usual cowboy tale, and will one day be recognized as such by filmmakers.

This thrilling and dramatic theme of survival against odds is one of the six reasons that we read *Arabia Deserta* today with the excitement that comes of great literature long after the factual information it conveys has become routine. Khalil has conquered other worlds as surely as the most intrepid astronaut of science fiction. Why has he done so? We can only guess. For ultimately, the question of motivation asked in the first sentence hovers over the entire book, a ghostly suspension which never finds resolution. Because of this unanswered question and its magic grammar, *Arabia Deserta* summons up in the reader an illusory, miragelike, almost hallucinatory feeling. Did Khalil ever indulge in hashish? We may never know, except for the narrator's disapproving reference to "brutish hemp smoking" (I, 151), but this knowledge might provide the secret key to the strange artistry and effect of the book. In any case, like Bunyan who promises in *Pilgrim's Progress* that "This book will make a traveller of thee," so Doughty has used his self and experiences to make his readers into deep voyagers.

CHAPTER 4

Travels in Arabia Deserta:
Characters and Scenes

DOUGHTY has set his ever-present if quiet protagonist Khalil against a rich background of varying characters and dramatic action. Although he fails to structure the book as a whole by imposing on it a framework other than his actual itinerary, we find that he has deliberately and consciously created a different kind of atmosphere in at least each of the major scenes by carefully amassing selected details and information. In these scenes, he makes use of the dramatic and character-building techniques known to all literary artists: selection and heightening of incident and dialogue and control of the narrator's perspective and revealed information. Barker Fairley is too extreme when he writes that "Doughty makes scant use of the common devices of story-tellers. . . . His book is in large measure amorphous in its art. . . ."[1] The structure of the book as a whole is indeed "amorphous"; but the structure of each great scene is decidedly not.

Although we cannot examine every character and event worthy of study in this enormous book, if we confine ourselves to the great scenes that every critic has found worthy of mention, we will see that in each one Doughty the artist has succeeded in projecting a different literary atmosphere. Thus, Khalil appears throughout as a unique variant on the Spenserian moral hero; the Medain Salih *kella* sequence is an example of fantastic Eastern narrative; Zeyd and Hirfa provide light domestic comedy; Mohammed Ibn Rashid is a high tragic hero; the town of Kheybar is portrayed in Gothic terms; the Aneyza merchant episode gives rise to an almost Trollopian satire; and the Salem-Fheyd climax is a unique example of adventure narrative combined with the literature of religious martyrdom. We see Doughty's range and ability as a writer to imitate several literary forms, like his idol Chaucer. And we gain an insight into why these characters and incidents will remain forever on the literary landscape.

91

I *Khalil*

Through the narrator's descriptions and Khalil's statements and actions, we have learned something of Khalil's multiple motivation, of his ideology of humility and painfully blunt speech, of his prejudices cloaked in universalism, his belief in technology, his irony when crossed, his adventurousness, and his bravery and dedication to his goals in difficult situations. But we see Khalil as a personality mainly through the eyes of his companions. The narrator never even grants us a direct description of Khalil's appearance, stature, or background. We learn what he looks like only by listening to some poor women speak about him: "Their women wondered to see the (English) colour of the stranger's hair; and said to one another, 'Is this a grey-haired man, that has tinged his beard with saffron?'—'Nay, thou mayest see it in his nature; this is certainly a red-man . . .'" (II, 443). The narrator forces us to put the pieces of the puzzle of Khalil's personality together from dialogue, the comments of other characters, and his own rare grants of insight, just as he forces us to guess at Khalil's motivation.

Nonetheless, the portrait of Khalil that emerges through the bits and pieces of his companions' comments is charming, particularly in the not infrequent moments of human weakness in which he is photographed as it were for all time. We emerge with perhaps less knowledge of him than of any other major character in English literature, but with a surprisingly solid opinion of what we *do* know. This is because Doughty has made the narrator emphasize five major qualities in Khalil: absentmindedness, reticence, honesty, caginess, and bravery.

Besides the dogmatism and bluntness which we have already discussed in the last chapter, his most apparent fault is absent-mindedness. This we witness when he is found sitting on a Koran by the prince at Hayil (I, 614) and when he continually and imprudently forgets the Moslem prayer hours (for example, II, 307). The narrator mentions Khalil's "incurable obliviousness" (II, 377), but the most human description of this trait comes to us through the mouth of Mohammed en Nejumy who got to know him well during the months at Kheybar:

"But who . . . can imagine any evil of Khalîl? for when we go out together, he leaves in one house his cloak or his driving-stick, and in another his agâl! he forgets his pipe, and his sandals, in other several houses. The strange negligence of the man! ye would say he is sometimes out of memory of the things about him! . . . but I am sorry Khalîl is so soon to leave us, for he is a sheykh in questions of religion, and besides a peaceable man." (II, 203)

Khalil's self-effacement, his lack of care of possessions, extends to his refusal to say much. As Aman the Galla puts it to him, "'I am a *Tourk* as thou art a Tourk: the Turks hold aloof from the people's levities'" (II, 118). Thus the following anecdote is the more amusing in its rare view of Khalil's sudden lack of stiffness and reticence:

When the Beduin friends insisted with me to let them see our holiday dance, I would not make a breach in their mirth, but, foreseeing their natural judgement, I was half-ashamed to show them the manner.—With that stern congruity which is in their wild nature, they found it light: "O!, what was that outlandish skipping and casting of the shanks, and this footing it to and fro!"—it seemed to them a morris dance!

We like Khalil because his faults seem minor in comparison with his virtues. The foremost of these virtues is his oaklike honesty, which the narrator portrays through such passages as: "I went only to the Kurdish Pasha ... who ... took me for a well-affected man that did nothing covertly" (I, 2); "Nejm and Mohammed Aly had boasted to them that the Nasrâny never lied, even were it to help himself ..." (I, 202). Despite his blunt honesty, Khalil can be subtly diplomatic, even manipulative, when he must: " ... I had passed over his fault, but I thought that to take it hardly was a necessary policy. Also the Arabs would have a man like the pomegranate, a bitter-sweet, mild and affectionate with his friends in security, but tempered with a just anger if the time call him ..." (I, 564). We do not see this caginess as a contradiction of his honesty, for we realize that Khalil had sometimes no choice but to manipulate his opponents during his struggle for survival, and the rarity of his choice of this method rather than frankness makes his honesty all the more apparent and daring.

Khalil's bravery comes across in his open confrontations with kings and brutal servants and hostile anti-Christians. The only element that daunts him is disease, and his fear remains powerfully moving: "Ten twilight days passed over me, and I thought, 'If the eyes should fail me!—and in this hostile land, so far from any good'" (I, 547); "Ah! what horror, to die like a rabid hound in a hostile land" (II, 452). But even these fears are set into a background of fact and event that abruptly shifts the reader's attention from them; there is no dwelling on them. We see in all these qualities why the Arabs "pardoned my person" even when they "thought me to blame for my religion" (I, 313), and why Khalil takes on a heroic Everyman quality.

Khalil comes across to the reader as his creator Doughty wanted him

to: as an unarmed and intelligent Spenserian knight who seeks moral
truth at any price. Khalil stumbles over his faults—like the Red Crosse
Knight—but they give his almost superhuman courage and self-control
a further believability. In studying the characters and scenes that follow, we must never forget the presence of this staunch knight in a
savage land.

II *Fabulous Eastern Narrative: Mohammed Aly and Haj Nejm in
the Kella at Medain Salih* (I, chapters 4–7, 13)

In this section of the book, the violent shifts of mood of the characters, the fabulous Eastern tales they (and the narrator) recount, and
Khalil's semidisappointing exploration of the Medain Salih monuments, are all of a piece. In the narrator's description of the *kella* and
its inhabitants, we seem to move in this our first lengthy contact with
Arabians, in a colorful Eastern fable in which nothing is quite what it
seems at first. The uncertain, shifting mental landscape reflects the
miragelike heat of the physical surroundings.

The narrator in this section of the book devotes great pains to warning us of this particular effect of the East: "Commonly the longer one
lives in a fabulous time or country, the weaker will become his judgement" (I, 173–74). He recounts the Syrian *Hâj* fables of the "Jews of
Kheybar," with their fantastic occurrences, tells of the rumor of there
existing two Christs in Syria in Khalil's time, and warns us of
Mohammed Aly's habit of multiplying every figure by ten when telling
his many tales. But as much as the narrator warns us and tries to bring
cold logic to bear on all these superstitious stories, we feel that Khalil
(and ourselves) are in a new Arabian Nights world where anything can
happen.

Khalil's exploration of the ruins at Medain Salih and Hejr is an
example of the way in which romance, reality, and differing perspec-
tives become unpleasantly intermingled in Arabia, as his view of the
ruins changes and contrasts with the Moslem view. The narrator
explains Khalil's first reaction to the monuments in the most excited
terms: "I mused what might be the sleeping riddle of those strange
crawling letters which I had come so far to seek!" (I, 106). But they are
disgustingly clouded over by flies: "Sultry was that mid-day winter sun,
glancing from the sand, and stagnant the air, under the sun-beaten
monuments; those loathsome insects were swarming in the odour of
the ancient sepulchres" (I, 107). These burial caves, which the narrator
tells us Khalil has risked his life to see, and of which he had such high

expectations, turn out to be only the work of "Semites, expeditious more than curious, and naturally imperfect workmen.—The interpretation of the inscriptions has confirmed these conjectures" (I, 115). When Khalil visits the monuments at el Hejr a third time, the narrator calls them "rat holes" set against "those ghastly grinning ranges of the Héjr" (I, 504), as D. G. Hogarth has pointed out. Khalil's and the narrator's own views have become subjective and unreliable. The monuments disappointed the romantic in Khalil. But in the Koran, Mohammed the Prophet presents them as proof of the ruin of idolators, as the narrator tells us with contempt (I, 95–96). The reader understands that each person may see something different in these monuments, as various people interpret differently the Marabar Caves in Forster's *A Passage to India*. As the narrator tells us in chapter 13 in an unusual insight influenced no doubt by his memory of the mirage atmosphere, "All things are much as we esteem them" (I, 369).

The narrator's characterization of Mohammed Aly and Haj Nejm has much in common with the expectation and disappointment and relative views of the monuments and the half-believable atmosphere of Eastern tales that he warns us against. The men appear first as Chaucerian "tower keepers," removed in time as well as space from our experience: "Mohammed Aly the kellâjy" and Haj Nejm, "an old Moor of Fez . . . was warden." Of the two, Mohammed Aly is the more violent and contradictory and therefore the more interesting to the narrator. He gives us a full two-page description informed by the retrospective knowledge of M. Aly's attack on Khalil, which, however, he keeps from us at this point:

The man, half ferocious trooper, could speak fair and reasonably in his better mind; then as there are backwaters in every tide, he seemed humane. . . . a tiger he was in his dunghill ill-humour. . . . his visage much like a fiend, dim with the leprosy of the soul and half fond; he shouted when he spoke with a startling voice, as it might have been of the ghrôl. . . . (I, 91)

The narrator has apparently exaggerated and "fabulized" Mohammed Aly's features with the use of medieval language and animal and supernatural metaphors. He forces us to see Mohammed Aly as a larger-than-life cartoon figure, and we only half-credit his description. The narrator's story about Mohammed Aly's "pulling out his scimitar" and cutting down "the rash unarmed slave" of the Hâj Pasha who accuses him of having stolen some of the Pasha's silver only adds to this unreal atmosphere (I, 92), as does Mohammed Aly's own wonderful

tale-telling ("we heard his tales for hours, all of good matter and elo-
quent . . . of the marrow of human experience" I, 126), including
exaggerations and wild oaths.

Mohammed Aly, with a voice like a *ghrôl* or specter, appears in the
narrator's initial description like a fiend out of his own tales, and we
doubt the description. Suddenly, in a moment of violence that erupts
from nowhere, the description turns out to be true as fantasy and reality come together. When Khalil demands the escort to the monuments
that M. Aly has promised in return for Khalil's carbine, and Khalil
insists on fulfillment of the promise rather than the return of his carbine, "the Moorish villain suddenly struck me with the flat hand and
all his mad force in the face, there wanted little of my falling to the
yard below. He shouted also with savage voice 'Dost thou not know me
yet?'" (I, 163). How can one "know" a *ghrôl*? When Khalil asks the
Beduin to witness this attack on a guest, the attacker gets even angrier
and strikes Khalil "with all his tiger's force" (I, 163) until Khalil the
passive must hold his wrists and say "'Now . . . have done, or else I am
a strong man'" (I, 164). M. Aly now threatens to kill Khalil but, in the
absence of a weapon, snatches his beard "with canine rage," pulling
him around the *kella*, "which is a most vile outrage" (I, 164).

As Melville has commented in "Bartleby the Scrivener" through his
lawyer narrator, nothing enrages an attacker as much as a passive
resistance. But even given this characteristic of Khalil's, the attack is
too savage, and we are not even given the reason for it at this point. In
a few more moments, Mohammed Aly becomes once again a "half
doting-religious and humane ruffian" (I, 165) and calls Khalil "*habîb*,"
or "a beloved." As irrationally and magically as he had attacked Khalil,
he becomes friends with him again, and only in small part is this owing
to Haj Nejm's sober warning about possible British reprisals.

The narrator only later tells us that Khalil found out that
Mohammed Aly thought the carbine not payment enough for his services, and expected some bargaining rather than firm insistence that
the agreement be fulfilled. This retrospective explanation scarcely jus-
tifies in our minds Mohammed Aly's extreme violence. We understand
that Khalil has stepped into an Eastern fable, outwardly attractive and
strange-beguiling but also false and dangerous. Because of the narrator's delayed-revelation technique, we suffer with Khalil the shock of
entering a game with new rules that must be painfully learned.

Doughty's message is that character, like landscape, in the East is
impossible to know or to trust, except in rare cases. Haj Nejm develops
in the first chapters of the *kella* story like a tolerant, reasonable, West-

ern man, who knows something of Europe. He raises vegetables quietly and greets Khalil and Zeyd warmly after their return to the tower in chapter 13. His killing of a man in his youth is described by the narrator as self-defense and not natural to Haj Nejm's character. Suddenly, because of Nejm's "quick sanguinary humour" (I, 371), we find him chasing his brother-in-law with a blunderbuss, while his assistant Hasan runs about yelling the Chaucerian-Arabic and therefore fairylike "'*Bess*, enough, 'nuncle, and now ho!'" (I, 372). Khalil concludes, as the narrator tells us, " . . . never to re-enter these sordid kella walls to lodge in them. . . . The same Haj Nejm, was to me always of an indulgent mildness. . . . But if upon a time there should fall any distaste between us . . . then certainly I had not long to live" (I, 373). Outwardly reasonable, even humane, characters suddenly justify their schizophrenic descriptions as monsters with a speed that startles even Khalil.

But as in his shifting view of the Medain Salih monuments, even the narrator is infected with this atmosphere of sudden about-face murderousness and forgiveness. As in a fairy tale, he abruptly turns our now well-founded fear of Mohammed Aly and Haj Nejm into human sympathy by blaming all on Islam and the Turkish government, claiming that "in some less iniquitous circumstance of things, and under a holier discipline of religion . . . Nejm might have been a saint also" (I, 373)! And on I, 502 and 511, Khalil does not hesitate to visit the *kella* and Nejm, who smiles warmly, again.

Doughty's very method of characterization in the *kella* section owes as much to Eastern influence as does his style. We emerge with pictures of the two men as cartoon figures who are remote and harmless, but who can erupt at any second into their Hyde-like opposites, no less than the "Jews of Kheybar" or "ghrols" or djinns. These characters would be fitting inhabitants of the "Dark Tower" to which Browning's Childe Roland came, had he wanted to populate it, or of one of Tolkien's dark towers full of changeable wizards. Our first contact with the East has been a very strange one, thanks to Doughty the artist's brilliant manipulation of our perceptions and old-masterly Dutch brush strokes of character.

III   Domestic Comedy: Zeyd and Hirfa of the Fukara Beduin
(I, chapters 8, 12)

In a comedy, we expect typed or half-rounded characters with one outstanding trait worthy of caricature, romantic problems, reversals of plot, and a happy solution. The narrator tells us of Khalil's involvement in "the comedy of Hirfa and Zeyd" (I, 231) in just these terms. Zeyd and Hirfa become prime, closely observed examples of the pleasures and pains of polygamy and Beduin love of trading that the narrator discusses anthropologically elsewhere in the chapters.

We first meet Zeyd in chapter 4 when Mohammed Aly recommends him to Khalil in an attempt to split the profits with Zeyd and thus pay off an old score between them:

... this nomad fox bestowed his sterile colt upon the Moorish wolf Mohammed Aly.... they both looked that I should pay the shot between them.... Zeyd was a swarthy nearly black sheykh of the desert, of mixed stature and middle age, with a hunger-bitten stern visage.... Zeyd uttered his voice in the deepest tones that I have heard of human throat; such a male light Beduin figure some master painter might have portrayed for an Ishmaelite of the desert. Hollow his cheeks, his eyes looked austerely, from the lawless land of famine ... where the chiefest Beduin virtue is ... a courageous forbearing ... of hunger.... A sheykh among his tribesmen of principal birth, he had yet no honourable estimation; his hospitality was miserable, and that is a reproach to the nomad dwellers of the empty desert.... nothing in Zeyd was barbarous and uncivil; his carriage was that haughty grace of the wild creatures. In him I have not seen any spark of fanatical ill-humour.... (I, 101–3)

Doughty presents a Beduin "noble savage" stereotype of Zeyd at the same time that he paints a very individual portrait of his looks, his prudence, and most of all of his un-Beduin miserliness, which is the quality that will be caricatured throughout. A "master painter" has already been at work creating a half-rounded character, and this picture escapes a tone of condescension because of its particularity within a generally typed framework.

As we learn soon after meeting her, Hirfa shares with Zeyd the miserly characteristics that make the pair famous in their tribe: "Hirfa, a sheykh's daughter and his nigh kinswoman, was a faithful make to Zeyd in all his sparing policy" (I, 222). She skimps on water (I, 218) and aids Zeyd in his attempt to hide in Khalil's hot little tent in order to avoid guests who would want to drink of his coffee (I, 223). Despite this thin cement, however, the pair has marital difficulties, as the narrator explains during his description of her character:

Hirfa was a sheykh's orphan, whom it seems he had taken partly for her few inherited camels. Hirfa was an undergrown thick Beduin lass, her age might be twenty.... Hirfa sighed for motherhood: she had been these two years with an husband and was yet ... "in her girlhood;" and she wept inwardly with a Semitic woman's grief. Zeyd and Hirfa were as Isaac and Rebecca; with the Beduin simplicity they sat daily sporting lovingly together before us, for we were all one family ... but oftentimes in the midst Hirfa pouted; then Zeyd would coldly forsake her, and their souls were anew divided. Hirfa in her weary spirit desired some fresh young husband, instead of this palled Zeyd, that she mistrusted could not give her children. (I, 230–31)

The situation of old husband and young wife has been hallowed comic material for centuries, and the narrator treats it in this case too as comedy rather than with full seriousness. His light descriptions of Hirfa make this clear: "Self-minded, a bold-faced wench, mistress Hirfa ..." (I, 231). To make the comic elements complete, he has even given us a chorus: "The comedy of Hirfa and Zeyd was become matter of daily raillery in the mejlis of the coffee-drinking sheukh their cousins ..." (I, 231).

Tales of Zeyd's wife-beatings become known and condemned, as against manly Beduin practice. But when Hirfa flees from Zeyd a second time, leaving him "in long heaviness of mind" (I, 232), "The common voice blamed Hirfa's second flight: 'How, they said, abandon Zeyd's tent in the presence of guests, and they were strangers!'—'Ha!' there answered an aged mother of our menzil to the old hind her husband, 'dost hear, Sâlih? The hareem be good for little now-a-days ...'" (I, 233). We might be listening to an old couple condemn current mores in any light Western comedy.

Khalil understands that as guest he must play go-between; but instead of convincing Hirfa to return with any moral or spiritual argument, he finds that he must give "the little peevish housewife" (I, 235) and all her family tobacco and thus buy her back. The ease of this transaction transforms a serious mission into fit material for laughter. Despite the narrator's overt, sentimental moralizing ("What oneness of hearts can be betwixt these lemans, whose lots are not faithfully joined?" I, 236) which might well suit popular comedy, we fail to sympathize with Hirfa in any serious way. We have been shown that she like Zeyd can be bought very easily, both being misers, and that if perhaps polygyny instead of polygamy were practiced, she would be no more reliable than Zeyd, elsewhere characterized by the narrator as "a smooth lover" (I, 237).

All's well that ends well, and our last view of the pair together, though not a resolution of their problem, is of Hirfa being teasingly courted by Khallaf Allayda while Zeyd "looked on manly and smiling" (I, 320) to see her praised. But the comedy is far from over as Doughty the artist provides a further comic reversal and climax. Zeyd still wants to unload Hirfa and offers her to Khalil. Khalil refuses to make the bad deal of taking Hirfa as a wife while leaving Zeyd with her camels:

. . . said Zeyd, " . . . hast thou any mind to be wedded amongst us? See, I have two wives and, billah, I will give thee to choose between them. . . . ." Perhaps he would have given me Hirfa, to take her again (amended) at my departure and in the meantime not to miss her camels; for it seemed he had married the orphan's camels. To this gentle proffer I answered, 'Would they needs marry me, then be it not with other men's wives, which were contrary to our belief. . . .' (I, 320–21)

Khalil defeats Zeyd's designs here; but Zeyd has the last laugh.

As might be expected, Khalil and Zeyd finally have a difference over payment for Zeyd's services and Khalil's camel. They settle the dispute but not before Khalil blunders in a Freudian slip of the tongue into calling Zeyd a *hablûs* or robber. Zeyd never forgets this insult in front of his sheikh, Motlog. They apparently make up, but Zeyd (no doubt remembering the insult and Khalil's refusal to take Hirfa) helps convince Khalil to pay ten reals and exchange his camel for another: "I bought thus upon their trust, a dizzy camel, old, and nearly past labour and, having lost her front teeth, that was of no more value, in the sight of the nomads, than my wounded camel. I was new in their skill . . ." (I, 355). In addition, Khalil even donates some of his needed clothing to the used-camel salesman because of the weeping of the man's wife. Thus, Khalil himself becomes a comic figure in the comedy of the Fukara. He has resisted Zeyd's attempt to sucker him with a bad wife, but gets "stung" by Zeyd on a camel deal instead. Hirfa, no doubt, had a good laugh with Zeyd, her fellow miser, about Khalil's naiveté in this business and in the tobacco she got him to give her when she would probably have come back again eventually anyway!

With real playfulness, Doughty the artist has revealed that Khalil is no match for the Beduin as the comedy of Hirfa and Zeyd becomes Khalil's comedy in the end. We see past the narrator's angry stricture that "the meditations of the Arabs are always of treachery" (I, 355) to the true fun of Khalil's having been caught out and made to join the human comedy.

IV   *High Tragedy: Mohammed Ibn Rashid at Court in Hayil*
(I, chapters 21–22; II, chapters 1–3)

Tragedy usually includes an aristocratic setting, a complex protagonist trapped by fate, and a cosmic justice which sets the disturbed balance caused by evil deeds right again. In recounting "the tragedies of the house of Ibn Rashîd" (II, 13), the narrator portrays all these elements brilliantly.

In a palace consisting of "lofty walls, painted in device with ochre and jiss" (I, 586–87), in which servants move about in "silken clothing" (I, 588), Khalil the blunt-spoken prophet confronts a brilliant and sophisticated court. Hamud, Mohammed Ibn Rashid's relative and adviser, whispers to Khalil about a problem of impotence "under the wing of his perfumed handkerchief" (I, 595), and is very proud of the English sword for which he paid "one thousand reals" and says "'It is excellent'" with the tone of a connoisseur. Like the other patricians of the court, he enjoys hunting and horse racing.

We are not surprised when Hamud exceeds Khalil (and the narrator) in delicacy and sophistication. Although the narrator calls him a "barbaric man" (I, 603) with a tone of superiority, Hamud conducts himself far more politely than Khalil. When Hamud asks simply if Khalil eats pork, Khalil violently responds, "'Ay billah, and that is not much unlike the meat of the wabar which ye eat, or of the porcupine. Do not the Beduw eat wolves and the hyena . . . but I would taste of none such'" (I, 603–4). Instead of justifiably castigating Khalil's second demonstration of incivility (the first is his lecturing Hamud about slavery, I, 603), Hamud merely answers quietly, "'My meaning was not to say, Khalîl, that for any filth or sickliness of the meat we abstain from swine's flesh, but because the Néby has bidden us'" (I, 604), and he goes on to further soothe his dinner guest by repeating that someone told his father that swine's flesh is "'very good meat'" (I, 604). In conducting himself as if he were superior to Hamud—behavior which Khalil would never have allowed himself in dealings with English aristocracy—Khalil has by contrast revealed his own clash-of-cultures arrogance and the polish of the Ibn Rashid court, a fitting setting for high tragedy.

If Hamud is a subtle character who reveals the delicacy of the court, Mohammed Ibn Rashid, the tragic hero of this episode, is far more interesting, delicate, and complex. For the first five hundred pages of the book, we hear only conflicting reports of him from the narrator. This mixed view is typical: "Bitter is the heart, and the sword is sharp, of him who rules over the wandering tribes of the khála! but in truth he might not else contain them" (I, 561). We get both moral condemnation and an extenuating judgment in the same sentence. When we finally meet him, we are in awe. The narrator informs us that Mohammed displays great courtesy by refusing to call Khalil the "reproachful name of Nasrâny" (I, 591), preferring the more polite "Mesîhy" instead, and we also learn that he "is said to be very well read in the Arabic letters, and a gentle poet" (I, 591), unexpected qualities in a feared ruler. He very intelligently pumps Khalil for his opinion of the Beduin sheikhs he has met and for Khalil's possible use as a healer and technologist. Later, he will presciently ask Khalil about the possible value of petroleum, how electricity works, and whether or not America was populated when the British colonized it, thus expressing his own suspicion of British colonialism. We learn, finally, that he is a good governor, which is the narrator's highest praise. As the narrator puts it later, "I think *it would be hard to find a fault in Ibn Rashîd's government*" (II, 32).

But Mohammed conceals many guilty secrets. Khalil is portrayed as the ascetic moral prophet Nathan confronting a guilty king David ("Tamar David's daughter" is even mentioned on II, 31) throughout this scene of his meeting with Mohammed. He lacks even sandals, and is compared to the "'prophets of Ullah'" (I, 593) by the old sheikh attending Ibn Rashid. As prophet, Khalil inadvertently fingers the king's guilt when Mohammed asks him to read from an Arabic history book:

> . . . with the impatient half-childish curiosity of the Arabians, the Emir Ibn Rashîd himself came over and sat down beside me.—"Where shall I read?"— "Begin anywhere at a chapter,—there!" and he pointed with his finger. So I read the place, '*The king* (such an one) *slew all his brethren and kindred.*' It was *Sheytân* [Satan] that I had lighted upon such a bloody text; the Emir was visibly moved! and, with the quick feeling of the Arabs, he knew that I regarded him as a murderous man. "Not there! he said hastily, but read here!—out of this chapter above" (beating the place with his finger); so I read again some passage. *Emir*: "Ha, well! I see thou canst read a little," so rising he went again to his place. (I, 591)

Through the narrator, Doughty portrays the Emir's guilty conscience in dramatic form, using action and dialogue and even indicating

"*Emir:*" as in a play. This is *Arabia Deserta*'s equivalent of Hamlet's play-within-a-play, with Khalil in the role of God's chosen instrument for exposing the bloody conscience of the king.

After revealing the king's guilt in this dramatic way, the narrator finally tells us the whole story. Prince Telal, ruler of Hayil, fell sick either naturally or because of poison and committed suicide to spare himself a long wasting disease that might have threatened his intelligence. Metaab, his wise and reasonable brother, ascended the throne, only to be assassinated by Telal's brutish eldest child, Bunder. Enticed back from Riyadh, to which he had fled when his brother Metaab had been killed, Mohammed Ibn Rashid discovered that he had been marked for death by Bunder. So Mohammed killed Bunder first, and then went on to eliminate all heirs who might pose a threat to him, regardless of age. He allowed some children to remain alive, surprisingly, Bunder's son among them.

But after portraying these events in brilliant and bloody style ("and with a murderous hand-cast he struck the blade into his nephew's bowels!" II, 16), the narrator exonerates Mohammed Ibn Rashid. Bunder, after all, wanted to kill Mohammed, and Bunder is one "whom no man mourned" (II, 26) because of his stupidity and brutality. Mohammed simply had no choice but to become a murderer:

Bunder slain, he must cut off kindred, which else would endanger him. The iniquity of fortune executed these crimes by Mohammed's hand, rather than his own execrable ambition.—These are the tragedies of the house of Ibn Rashîd! Their beginning was from Telâl, the murderer of himself: the fault of one extends far round, such is the cursed nature of evil, as the rundles of a stone dashed into water, trouble all the pool. (II, 16)

We see Mohammed as the victim of the "iniquity of fortune" or Fate itself, which placed him in the middle of an irreversible chain of murders to which he was forced to contribute in simple self-defense and as an act of just revenge for his brother's death.

But as a tragedian, Doughty is not satisfied without suggesting cosmic justice in operation. Mohammed may have been trapped, he may even have executed just revenge, but he has still murdered innocent children and become himself a tyrant, and must pay a price. So the narrator stresses the fact that Mohammed is sterile: "his children are as dead within him, and the dreaded inhabitant of yonder castle remains a desolate man, or less than a man, in the midst of his mar-

riages" (II, 26). Because he can produce no heir, Mohammed has been
forced to let some of his dead rivals' children live. And because of this
necessity, the whole family is doomed: some of the children already
hate one another. Two children are even half-brothers who have had
the same mother, but whose respective fathers are victim and murderer! It is clear that, as in some Faulknerian family, the future history
will be as bloody and tragic as the past: "O God! who can forecast their
tragedies to come!" (II, 27), says the narrator, warming to his theme.
He further predicts the finish of the whole line of Ibn Rashids: "Now
first the lordship of Shammar is fully ripe: after such soon-ripeness we
may look for rottenness, as men succeed of less endowments to admin-
ister that which was acquired of late by warlike violence, or when this
tide of the world shall be returning from them" (I, 618). We are
assured in very Shakespearean tones that a bloody regime will be fore-
closed by the powers of the universe. And in fact, the Wahabi Ibn
Sauds severely defeated the Ibn Rashids in battle in 1906 and went on
by 1926 to consolidate all of Saudi Arabia (including the Hejaz, which
was controlled by the Hussein family), eliminating the rival dynasty in
the process!

In this episode, Doughty as tragedian has shaped the bare if sensational outlines of history into the grandeur, entrapment by fate, and
cosmic justice of a Renaissance revenge drama. But the final complexity of Mohammed as a character appears only much later in the book.
Khalil was roughly expelled from Hayil. (No reason is given by the
narrator, but we assume the expulsion is a result of Khalil's European
arrogance, the hostility of the ignorant population of Hayil, and
Mohammed's suspicions of colonialism combined.) We would expect
Khalil to regard Mohammed as evil after this poor treatment. But
when in Tayif near the end of the whole story, when he has long ago
taken leave of Mohammed, Khalil is asked by the Sherif whether he
takes Mohammed "'for a good man.'" And Khalil surprisingly renders
this reply: " . . . I answered a little beside his expectation, 'He is a worthy man . . . '" (II, 510). Even Khalil himself, after his own narrow
escapes and fateful encounters, concludes that Ibn Rashid is more
tragic than sinful despite his own bad experience with him. This final,
delayed judgment of Khalil's cements the already complex and unforgettable portrait rendered by the narrator. Because of his strong belief
in a religious order in the universe and his deep artistic sympathy, even
with the dictator Ibn Rashid, Doughty—by manipulating dialogue,
narrator's perspective, and the arrangement of his material—has been

able in this episode to do what no other writer of his century succeeded in accomplishing: he creates true tragedy. He revives broken literary forms as well as a language he considers weakened.

V   Gothic: Abdullah the Commandant and Mohammed en Nejumy at Kheybar (II, chapters 3–8)

In the great Kheybar section of his book, Doughty displays an ability to create a Poe-like Gothic atmosphere, complete with warlocks, werewolves, witches, djinns, hemp-smoking dervishes, and the horror of Khalil's captivity and possible death at the hands of the brutal and corrupt Turkish jailer, Abdullah el Siruan. Khalil was bitterly disappointed when he found that the fabulous Kheybar that he had risked his life to find was no more than a foul village of superstitious peasants: "But let none any more jeopardy his life for Kheybar!" (II, 127) says the narrator. But Doughty the artist turned this typical Arabian-traveler disillusionment into a reverse romance of heavy presentiments, deformed personalities, and evil odors and thoughts.

The journey to Kheybar—like the opening journey of Poe's "Fall of the House of Usher"—is difficult, not only because unfaithful guides attempt to abandon Khalil en route, but because of a foreboding natural atmosphere: "We mounted in the morrow twilight; but long after daybreak the heavens seemed shut over us, as a tomb, with gloomy clouds" (II, 71). The goal finally in sight, Khalil has a sense of coming evil which finds support in the evil landscape of the village:

Foul was the abandoned soil upon either hand, with only few awry and undergrown stems of palms. The squalid ground is whitish with crusts of bitter salt-warp . . . and stained with filthy rust. . . . How strange are these dank Kheybar valleys in the waterless Arabia! A heavy presentiment of evil lay upon my heart as we rode in this deadly drowned atmosphere. (II, 76)

Kheybar is Khalil's "Heart of Darkness," and like Conrad's, it reflects an African setting: "Kheybar is as it were an African village in the Hejâz" (II, 77). The narrator uses the blackness of the Kheybarians' skin as a metaphor for the blackness of their hearts in a way that may prove distasteful to some modern readers. But in this case it should be said in his defense that he points out that there is another Negro village which is far more liberal than Kheybar (II, 100), el Hayat, and that the moral "blackness" of Kheybar is uniquely its own.

We slowly learn that every possible superstition exists in this village: dream interpretation, a senseless refusal to eat leeks and chickens, belief in witches, belief in Christians' power to find treasure, and belief that Christians rose from the sea. Just as the people of Kheybar bar themselves into their houses at night for fear of witches, so they are barred in mentally by their ignorance, physically by the disease of the town, and politically by the corrupt and tyrannous rule of the Dowla, or Turkish government, represented by Abdullah and his bully Sirur. Khalil's captivity in this medieval setting serves as an emblem of the villagers' captivity: he regresses into the Middle Ages and gets too real a taste of those times. No wonder that, as in a horror film, Khalil's guide, the otherwise brave Ghroceyb, wants to leave him at the edge of the town and run away, while the naive Khalil insists upon entering! And the first white man Khalil meets in Kheybar, Ahmed, immediately denounces him to Abdullah.

Despite Khalil's incredulous and mocking view (II, 107) of the villagers' superstitious stories, the narrator reports that "There were few at Kheybar that could not tell of some night's fearful jeopardy of their precious soul and body" (II, 107) because of witches. And he reports in great detail (II, 188–94) many marvelous (and scary) djinn tales and other fabulous stories of the villagers, thus further heightening this atmosphere for the reader. Although Khalil apparently maintained his "scientific" detachment to the last, could he have remained entirely aloof from the fear inspired by such beliefs in almost everyone around him, including his normally skeptical friend Mohammed en Nejumy, who thinks djinns real even as he denies the existence of witches?

If Khalil could continue to challenge and mock the villagers' "dark" fears, he noticed very clearly the real horror of the place, "the dreadful blackness of all things at Kheybar" (II, 81), as the narrator informs us: "I daily wondered to see almost no young children in Kheybar! The villagers answered me, 'The children . . . die in this air!—it is the will of Ullah'" (II, 110). The town is infested with a chronic fever. Aman, Khalil's African companion, is sick with tuberculosis, and Muharram, an Albanian soldier, dies of fever while Khalil is in the city, and has even his "dirty linen" auctioned off grotesquely by Abdullah, as the narrator tells us with loathing. In short, "'Kheybar, said the melancholy Aman . . . is . . . the whole world's sepulchre'" (II, 126). Even Amm Mohammed, Khalil's friend, has a syphilitic disease which has entered the dormant stage, and has infected his own brother Ahmed with it. To make matters worse, each year when the *Hâj* returns from Mecca, the town fears a cholera epidemic (II, 177), and when Khalil tries to relax in nature, he notices huge rats in the garden! (II, 120). We might call this section of the book "Death in Kheybar," or "The Plague." Doughty is as great an artist of the plague metaphor as Boccacio, Pepys, Defoe, Manzoni, Poe, Camus, and Mann.

More deadly than the plague itself remains the human plague of the Turks and the ignorant townspeople who oppress Khalil, the physician who might cure them if they would let him. Not only must he fear disease, the threat of which increases with the duration of his captivity in the town, but he actually is in danger of execution. This is only one of the evils stemming from Abdullah's corrupt government. The villagers say of the Turks "ALL THEIR BUSINESS IS RAPINE," but having invited them to rule in place of Ibn Rashid, Kheybar's Sheikh Salih cannot get rid of them because Ibn Rashid would then reenter and punish him. This forced rule of the Dowla, which the people have called down on themselves, even perverts the Beduins' own tribal ties. In a passage entitled "Unnatural Tribesmen," we read that Beduin enrolled as Abdullah's soldiers fired on their own tribesmen during a Beduin attack on the town: "'We that eat the bread of the Dowla must fight for the Dowla, even against our own people . . . '" (II, 105).

Abdullah, whose name is mentioned first in italics, like that of a character in a list of dramatis personae, is a "hypocrite" (II, 86) who pretends to maintain order while he steals all he can from his own men and from the people of the town. When he searches Khalil, he takes his six pounds for "'better keeping'" (II, 84). Worse, he toys with Khalil's life constantly, keeping him in deliberate fear. His toady Sirur "bellows . . . 'we will send to the Pasha; and if the Pasha's word be to cut his head off, we will chop off thy head Nasrâny'" (II, 84). For most of Khalil's three and a half months in this town, he was kept under this uncertain and therefore unbearable fear, that the Pasha in Medina would write Abdullah to execute him, as the narrator tells us: "These were days for me sooner of dying than of life; and the felonous Abdullah made no speed to deliver me" (II, 128). And the superstitious townspeople are little better: they actually shoot at Khalil (and miss) once and cast "their bitter eyes" (II, 83) on him. In their "panic terror," they think Khalil is "a warlock, come to bewitch their village" (II, 91).

The one bright spot in this very dark tapestry ("All is horror at Kheybar!" II, 79) remains Mohammed en Nejumy, Khalil's one friend and protector: "He was of a mild and cheerful temper, confident, tolerant, kind, inwardly God-fearing, lightly moved: his heart was full of a pleasant humour of humanity" (II, 112). For all his good qualities, however, Amm Mohammed too has his "Kheybarish" faults: besides syphilis, he has contracted Kheybar fever; he strikes his wife and son even as he is good to the guest; he believes in djinns even as he mocks witches; he, like Abdullah, wants Khalil to find riches; and he sometimes weakens in his defense of Khalil: "The Nejûmy, who stood as a looker-on to-day among us, was loud and raw in his words; and gave his counsel so fondly before them all, and manifestly to my hurt! that I turned from him with a heartache. The traveller should sail with every fair wind in these fanatical countries, and pass forth before good-will grow cold . . ." (II, 213). Mohammed says a private and friendly good-bye to Khalil and refuses to accept any money for his hospitality, but we see the taint of Kheybar in his character here and in similar passages (II, 136, 202).

Finally, the Pasha (whose name should be remembered for his goodness, but is not by an artist apparently bent on presenting only ill experience of Kheybar) decides on Khalil's release. Even the "slave-hearted Abdullah began now to call me 'Uncle Khalîl'" (II, 211). He is afraid that Khalil will tell the Pasha about his attempted robbery of Khalil's money and physical attack on Khalil when he attempted to reclaim it (II, 201). But Khalil's St. Paul role wins out in the end, as justice is miraculously done. Just as he took Abdullah's slap without violence (and did not respond to Mohammed Aly's blow in the *kella*), so he forgives his enemies when he leaves: "Although I had suffered wrong, I said to them (to the manifest joy of the guilty Abdullah) the last word of Peace" (II, 214). When he has made the villagers a new well (II, 197) and preached Christian forgiveness to Mohammed en Nejumy (II, 148) during his own troubles, he has remained faithful to the turning of the other cheek demonstrated throughout the book— and has received his goods and money back as well. Like the crucifix held before Dracula, Khalil's Christianity has once again demonstrated its power by taking him through the most Gothic circumstances unscathed.

Nonetheless, he knows that other Christians have not been so fortunate, like the man murdered by a Moslem soldier whose story he tells in this section of the book. The narrator's gasp "oh joy! this sun being fairly risen, the abhorred landmarks of Kheybar appeared no more" (II, 217) expresses Khalil's feelings when leaving the town. Like Poe's narrator of the Usher tale, he is glad to be alive, having narrowly escaped the clutches of the djinns, witches, and physically and mentally deformed human monsters of Kheybar.

VI   *Satire: Abdullah el Bessam and Abdullah el Kenneyny at
         Aneyza* (II, chapters 12–15)

"Satire" refers to the literary ridicule, mild or sarcastic, of the follies
of society. As society doctor and then outcast in the Aneyza episode of
Arabia Deserta, Khalil sees the faults of the Arabian town at first hand.
As idealized Good Physician he maintains his role of Christian sufferer
throughout his decline and fall from high social standing, meekly asking "'what need of violence?'" (II, 404) even as he is expelled. But the
retrospective narrator has not forgotten any insult and has avenged all
of Khalil's social sores with a wickedly sharp scalpel which he applies
to the skin of Arab society. So while Khalil's turning of the other cheek
only elicits more buffets until he is finally helped to leave the town for
good, the narrator uses Khalil's experiences to reveal and condemn the
faults of Islam and Khalil's inconstant friends. The narrator's targets
are greed and religious intolerance, and his satire begins as a mild and
playful Axel-Muntheian or Trollopian irony but becomes, as Khalil
falls, a Breughel-like sharpness and bitterness of vision. Khalil's role of
saintly scapegoat reveals Arabian man's—and all men's—foolishness,
wickedness, and most of all, greed, even in Khalil's closest friends, as
the narrator points the lesson for us in no uncertain terms.

At first, when the town's ruler Zamil and the people receive Khalil
well, providing him with an enthusiastic clientele for his medical practice, the narrator, in a section entitled "The Town Manners" (II, 349),
offers an attractive picture of trade, the main occupation of the town,
despite his usual class disapproval of merchants:

> The tradesmen's shops are well furnished. . . . Dates . . . are very good here;
> and nearly 30 pounds were sold for one real. . . .
> There is an appearance of welfare in the seemly clothing of this towns-
> folk. . . . (II, 348–49)

The narrator's good humor extends even to Islam at this point, as he
gives us his most positive description of it to be found anywhere in the
book:

> Mohammed's sweet-blooded faith has redeemed them from the superfluous
> study of the World, from the sour-breathing inhospitable wine; and has pur-
> ified their bodies from nearly every excess of living. . . . Marriage is easy from
> every man's youth; and there are no such rusty bonds in their wedlock, that
> any must bear an heavy countenance. The Moslem's breast is enlarged; he

finds few wild branches to prune of his life's vine,—a plant supine and rich
in spirit, like the Arabic language. There is a nobility of the religious virtue
among them, and nothing stern or rugged, but the hatred of the kafir: few
have great hardness in their lives. (II, 349)

Aside from the one bitter thorn about hatred of non-Moslems, it
appears that Islam—including its marriage and divorce customs!—has
won the narrator's respect here, as he reflects Khalil's good treatment.
   Khalil wins acquaintance with the big merchants of the town,
Abdullah el Bessam and Abdullah el Kenneyny, and eats well with
them (in contrast to his usual hunger) while he enjoys talks about contemporary politics and finance very similar to the mercantile or political chat of a Trollope novel. The narrator's satire or criticism of the
mores of these merchants is very good-natured now:

We sit at leisure at the European board, we chat cheerfully; but such at the
Arabs' dish would be a very inept and unreasonable behaviour!—he were not
a man but an homicide, who is not speechless in that short battle of the teeth
for a day's life of the body. And in what sort (forgive it me, O thrice good
friends! in the sacrament of the bread and salt,) a dog or a cat laps up his
meat, not taking breath, and is dispatched without any curiosity, and runs
after to drink; even so do the Arabs endeavour, that they may come to an
end with speed. . . . (II, 352)

   But the preaching of the public ministers begins to incite the population against its Christian doctor, and Khalil's less-faithful acquaint-
ances begin to shun him. Even "The Kenneyny would not be marked
to harbour a Nasrâny . . ." (II, 376), as the narrator informs us. On II,
372–74 the narrator can still give us his most approving universal statement on Islam, saying that Moslems "as the rest of mankind" (II, 372)
are "nearly irrational in matter of faith." But Khalil's visit to an intolerant priestly relative of the Bessam family suddenly provokes the narrator's most venomous attack on Mohammed and Islam in the whole
book:

. . . for the . . . virtues that were in him . . . cannot amend our opinion of the
Arabian man's barbaric ignorance, his sleight and murderous cruelty . . . or
sweeten our contempt of an hysterical prophetism and polygamous living. . . .
Sword is the key of their imagined paradise. . . . The Arabian religion of the
sword must be tempered by the sword: and were the daughter of Mecca and
Medina led captive, the Moslemîn should become as Jews! (II, 378–79)

While Khalil preaches to the Aneyzans that "'Every creature is *rasûl Ullah!*'" (II, 380), or a messenger of God, deserving respect, the narrator utters an entirely different message.

Although the narrator exonerates El Bessam and El Kenneyny from religious intolerance, we now begin to hear from him direct disapproval of their business practices which Khalil never voices and which the narrator himself has overlooked before. He reports a poor farmer's words, "'Seest thou yonder camels?—they are the Bessàm's; and nearly all this corn will be theirs to pay for their loan; and we must every year borrow afresh from them'" (II, 387), and sums up by terming Bessam-type usury a "kind of human malice" (II, 388). We learn for the first time now that El Kenneyny built up his fortune in the slave trade, and that even now he maintains an unscrupulous horse-trading business based on "the wealthy ignorance of foreign buyers" (II, 390). Although "Silver" was "for the Kenneyny in his philosophical hours . . . 'world's dross'; nevertheless the merchant . . ." now hesitates before cashing Khalil's bank draft and tells Khalil, "'Trust not . . . to any man! not even to me'" (II, 418). The narrator's use of the term "the merchant" for Kenneyny in the above quotation reveals ironic contempt.

And when Khalil remains outside Aneyza, having finally been expelled by a weak Zamil unable to overrule his council, his friends do not visit him, as the narrator tells us: " . . . there came none of my acquaintance to visit the Nasrâny. Their friendship is like the voice of a bird upon the spray: if a rumour frighten her she will return no more" (II, 441). Hamed el Yayya, the Arabian of "good family" whom the narrator had approved because his family "had never put their hands to merchandise" (II, 383), comes to see Khalil only as he is about to leave, using "glozing . . . words" (II, 453) to excuse himself, promises to come again to say good-bye, and never shows up.

Although El Kenneyny and El Bessam do fulfill their promise to send Khalil forward and wish him good-bye, he has seen very little of them during his times of trouble, and we see that they are less than full friends and furthermore that they are unprincipled in business. In contrast to the Beduin, whose sharp dealing is forgiven by the narrator because of their poverty, these rich men who live off the poor are not spared, as we have seen. In a subtly ironic thrust, the narrator tells us that El Kenneyny "was of the best kind of spirits, or next to the best" (II, 362). Although he remembers their kindness, the narrator lacks Khalil's idealized self-effacement, and like a Dutch master has left us with a crystal clear and merciless portrait of the inner social faults of the well-dressed merchants and all classes of Aneyza townspeople.

VII   *Adventure and Denouement: Salem, Fheyd, the Sherif of*
        Mecca and Khalil in Jidda (II, chapters 16–18)

In these chapters, the narrator presents a climax of dramatic action
and a contrasting peaceful if ironic denouement to the whole adventure. The sensational metaphors and powerful action of the Salem-
Fheyd incident are followed by subtle and symbolic ironies as Doughty
the artist, through the narrator, purposely builds dramatic tension and
relief.

Khalil leaves Aneyza with a caravan headed for Mecca. He as a
Christian will not be allowed in or near Mecca, and he expects that the
people El Kenneyny and El Bessam have instructed to protect him will
provide a connecting caravan or guide to Jidda. Instead, he finds that
they have provided nothing, and "I was now to pass a circuit in whose
pretended divine law is no refuge for the alien . . . and where any felon
of theirs in comparison with a Nasrâny is one of the people of Ullah.
I had looked to my pistol in the night . . ." (II, 484).

In this section of the book, the narrator gives us unusually frequent
and close reports of Khalil's thoughts and changes of mood, so we
become involved closely in the action. As always, the narrator's landscape reflects Khalil's feelings: "The aspect of this country is direful.
We were descending to Mecca—now not far off—and I knew not by
what adventure I should live or might die on the morrow" (II, 477–
78). Later, after leaving Tayif on the way to Jidda, safe passage assured
by the Sherif and justice done, Khalil heads back through the same
area and the narrator writes: "This third time I must remeasure the
long valley to 'Ayn ez-Zeyma: to-day it seemed less direful, since I rode
in the sun of the Prince's favour" (II, 529).

On the uncertain way to Mecca, Khalil's feelings are rendered in the
narrator's best Gothic tones. A camel falls and puts his leg out of joint,
and the narrator gives us a graphic account of how the camel is cut up
for meat, since this accident has no remedy, and then suddenly transforms this description into a metaphor for Khalil's situation: "Between
the fall of the thelûl, and an end of their butchery, the caravan camels
had not marched above two hundred paces!— . . . I thought, in few
minutes, my body might be likewise made a bloody spectacle" (II,
485). When the caravan stops at the first coffeehouse in the Mecca
country in order to leave Khalil there, he hears a "savage voice" (II,
485) call for his forcible conversion to Islam, and then hears another
"voice of ill augury" and meets the knife-wielding "fiend" (II, 486)

Salem, the robber-sheikh. Abandoned by the false son of El Bessam, who was assigned by his father to protect Khalil, Khalil like a true hero moves coolly, "without show of reluctance" (II, 486), as if confronting a mad dog. But the narrator gives us a heightened, adventure-romance description of Khalil's inner feelings in this view of the camel men surrounding Salem and himself: "Those Mecca faces were black as the hues of the damned, in the day of doom: the men stood silent, and holding their swarthy hands to their weapons" (II, 486). In similar heightened tones, the narrator tells us of Khalil's psychological and physical strategy in the confrontation with the Salem who "made feints with the weapon at my chest" (II, 487).

Frustrated by Khalil's outward lack of fear and by the verbal defense of Khalil by Maabub, a servant of the Sherif of Mecca who is quartered at Tayif, Salem settles for robbing items of clothing which Khalil passively lets go. Khalil's passive reversal of the swashbuckling role of the usual adventure tale is mirrored by an unusual twist of the plot: Maabub actually charges Salem with Khalil's safety. He will go under Salem's guidance to Tayif for a judgment by the Sherif: "Thus, Maabûb who had appeased the storm, committed me to the wolf. . . . Maabûb left me with the mad sherîf!" (II, 489).

After making sure we have noticed this unique situation, the narrator never lets us forget Khalil's danger for a moment: "But what that miscreant rolled in his lunatic spirit concerning me I could not tell: I had caught some suspicion that they would murder me in this place . . ." (II, 493). By careful manipulation and Christian passivity, Khalil just barely controls the situation. The narrator dramatizes with a series of questions Khalil's thoughts in the climactic moment when he must decide to shoot Salem and his cohort Fheyd, or give up his pistol: "What should I do now? . . . I thought, Shall I fire? . . . and if I could break away . . . what then?" (II, 496). Khalil decides to render the pistol and receives only a blow from a heavy camel stick that sends him reeling. In a perfect rendition of mob psychology, the narrator now describes Salem's friendly gestures. He has taken Khalil's things and has had his lust for sadistic pleasure satisfied, so we hear in his dialogue an insidious wheedling: "'Ha! Khalîl, we are become brothers; Khalîl, are we not now good friends? there is nothing more betwixt us'" (II, 499).

After more taunts and threats, which Khalil like a true hero parries coolly ("'I have not so lived, Moslêm, that I must fear to die,'" II, 502), they arrive at Tayif. Although the physical aspect of Tayif is gloomy, "after nigh two years' wandering in the deserts" climaxed by recent dangers, the town "was a wonderful vision" (II, 505) for Khalil. The narrator portrays it like the heavenly city, where Khalil is miraculously greeted by the "gentle thoughts of the homely humanity of the Prince of Mecca" (II, 506) and "anointed" and attired in white like a martyred saint. As St. Paul, Khalil forgives all his enemies before the just Sherif, calling Ibn Rashid a "'worthy man'" (II, 510) and asking only the return of his things from Salem. Even Salem thanks Khalil for his mercy (II, 514). The Sherif turns out to be "a natural Arabian Prince" and a "pleasant" pipe-smoking man, much like an English aristocrat, who offers Khalil tea and safe conduct to Jidda (II, 509) or other parts of Arabia, and promises to punish Salem.

For all this good treatment and intelligent talk, the narrator drives home one bitter message of Khalil's journey: "between them and us is brittle ground" (II, 520–21). Despite the tolerance of good men like the Sherif, the cultures cannot be bridged. Only political expediency in the end remains. The Sherif is as worried about British retaliation for molestation of Khalil as he is about Khalil's personal safety and comfort. Under the romance of Arabia remains one harsh reality, which the reader sees more clearly than the narrator or Khalil: each people constructs a false romance about the other based on fear and myth, and a true appreciation is very hard to attain.

Khalil is not equipped, by his very nature, to close the cultural gap. But despite himself he carries away an unforgettable attraction to the desert. Only illness prevents Khalil from trying to "unriddle that enigma" (II, 524) of the Empty Quarter, and the narrator reports of Khalil, somewhere between irony and seriousness, that on the way to Jidda a sheikh "read it, in my eyes, that I was nigh of heart to the Moslemîn" (II, 534).

On the very last page of the book, Doughty the artist, through the narrator, has ironically and symbolically summed up the meaning of the whole adventure in a few brief and ostensibly innocent brushstrokes whose import has been overlooked by previous critics. For his entry into Jidda, Khalil is decked out in the Sherif's clothing as an "emir el-Aarab" (II, 539). His appearance is certainly ironic if we remember his negative views of the Arabs expressed throughout the book, but truthful and appropriate if we see him as a prince of the spirit who has survived the harshest human and physical trials that the desert—and British official governmental indifference—could mete out.

The narrator bitingly mocks the "vanity of their religion" (II, 539) and Arab fabulizing, which makes Moslems claim to have found the grave of Eve near Jidda and transforms a merchant's grandiloquent house into a "Sherîf's palace" (II, 539) at a word, but he has some irony left for the British as well. Far from quietly anticlimactic, the final sentence ("On the morrow I was called to the open hospitality of the British Consulate") brings us back to the first page of the book with stinging effect. There the British consul in Damascus had forsaken Khalil by refusing to provide him with the passport that might have made the difference between good or bad treatment. The narrator mentions incidentally (II, 514) that the Jidda British consulate has forsaken another Englishman in Arabia, just as Khalil was forsaken. Here on the last page, this same Jidda consulate, no better than the Damascene one, calls Khalil to its "open hospitality" upon his arrival in Jidda. Now the British government is pridefully eager to claim the hero it had abandoned (like a treacherous Beduin guide) earlier and whose work it had impeded.

Loyalty, truth, and honor are rare qualities among both British and Arabs, as Prince Khalil alone is in a position to appreciate. Despite his faults, Khalil alone has maintained absolute integrity among all the characters of the book. Seen against this background of treachery and moral failure, he remains with all his admitted and unadmitted faults a unique and strangely human hero. For all the narrator's reticence, we find Khalil at the end curiously close and dear to us. We would not wish him—or the brave, weak, humane, and vicious characters who have brought out his heroic traits—any other way.

Arabia is now known, thanks to the explorations of Doughty and his predecessors and followers. But his rich, deep portrait, like the painting of a Breughel who wandered into nineteenth-century Arabia and left an indelible record of its inhabitants, its landscape, and most of all himself, will endure forever, because it transcends the surface of its subject and reaches deep into the human mystery with the insight, structuring, inexhaustibility, and universality of art.

CHAPTER 5

Pilgrim's Progress:
The Dawn in Britain, Adam Cast Forth, Mansoul

I Victorian Gothic

DOUGHTY'S major poetry reveals the continued progress of his spiritual pilgrimage into the past, as well as his conscious and more usual religious and political attitudes; no consideration of his mind can be complete without it. But it cannot be compared in literary stature to *Arabia Deserta*, one of the world's notable books. *Arabia Deserta's* radical originality of style and content arises from the exotic reality of its true journey. Its use of Arabic words and rhythms and biblical parallelism, combined with Chaucerian phrases, is unique and appropriate for the story and characters. Its characters are human because of their lovable and unlovable idiosyncrasies and faults, its digressive structure acceptable because of its reflection of Doughty's actual wanderings. In his absentmindedness, bluntness, courage, and strange sweetness, Khalil resembles no previous hero and appears all too human and fallible when pitting his own prejudices against those of the Arabs. The narrator's prejudices too are modified and undercut by the Arab characters' defense of their position, which he reports, and he, like Khalil, shows the effects of a subtle influence of the East.

The major poetry—outside of *Adam Cast Forth*—unfortunately displays less original and complex qualities. In *Dawn in Britain* (1906–1907), Doughty's 30,000 line epic of early Britain, conventional epic models supply ten syllable lines, clichéd major heroes and undifferentiated minor ones, sentimental heroics and villainy, unmodified Victorian British imperialist and Christian partisanship, and a neo-epic style which is occasionally powerful but used regardless of its appropriateness in each incident, like a straitjacket wrapped around content.

116

While writing *Dawn*, Doughty forgot what he learned in Arabia, that idealized dreams of the past and actual reality are bound to be in conflict. He could not qualify in the made-up poetry the simpleminded idealization of his narrow patriotic and religious beliefs, as Khalil's companions drawn from real life persistently counter his. No character ever makes a real case for the "other side" in Doughty's poetry. The speaker of *Dawn*—like the speakers of all Doughty's narrative poetry—has all the *Arabia Deserta* narrator's prejudices pressed to an extreme of violence and sentimentality, and so do the characters. Since there is no modifying semiconscious artist to differentiate from the narrative voice, we will call all his poetic speaker-artists "Doughty," with no need for finer distinctions. Finally, *Dawn* lacks a sense of proportion, being filled with too many minor characters and too much eminently forgettable action.

Mansoul (1920; revised 1923) is a more gentle and relaxed, even luminous, poem—except for a patriotic outburst against the kaiser—but this meditative epic of 240 pages is also narrated by a boring Victorian Doughty who utters ponderous clichés of low-level philosophy as if they were new discoveries, and contains characters who are one-dimensional and vapid and who, as in the case of *Dawn*, agree completely with the speaker's views. As poet, Doughty simply lacks the deep insight into and sympathy with character displayed by the artist of *Arabia Deserta* and all poets whom we would call great. Only in the short lyric drama *Adam Cast Forth* (1908) do we hear an authentic autobiographical note of desert suffering and deep sensory perception rendered in a style that makes the characters live, and there is no dogmatic or sentimental narrative voice to spoil this.

In *Mansoul*, Doughty openly compares his poetry to a Gothic cathedral:

> His énranged rampant buttresses, meetly upbear;
> Each one, a gracious work of masons craft,
> · (Pleasant to look upon;) his Fanes long flanks.
>   Within, the great Cathedral-structure rests
> On álligned clustered pillars' striding arcs:
> Their chapitérs graced with graven lily flowers
> And palms; whose spandrels deckt with effigies are,
> Of blesséd wights; that beckon down to us,
> Of righteous paths: whose walling, white, above;
> Gem-like, lo, ancient storied windows pierce;
> Radiant with purple joy of Heavens light.

> And cieled all is with vault of sculptured stone;
> Of noble aspect, like to palm-leaf work.[1]

In the style as well as the content of this passage, which is notable for its success, in contrast to many of Doughty's other poetic attempts to recapture the past, we note the lovingly-culled archaic words and coinages ("enranged," "upbear," "wights"), the absence of possessive apostrophes ("masons," "Fanes"), the use of precise, craftsmanlike terminology ("chapiters," "spandrels"), the archaic spelling ("deckt"), the attention to vegetative detail ("graven lily flowers / And palms"), the use of hallowed poeticism ("lo"), the archaically hyphenated words ("Gem-like"), the inversions and clogged, rough movement caused by an excess of punctuation, the simple, direct aesthetic sensibility ("Pleasant to look upon"), the dwelling on concrete objects, the delicately placed (one is tempted to say hand-placed) accent marks, which appear artlessly obvious, and of course the simple and unquestioning religious feeling ("righteous paths," "purple joy of Heavens light"), all of which succeed in recapturing the charmingly rough and fresh feeling of the Middle Ages and serve as a concrete demonstration of Doughty's ability as a poetic "maker" or craftsman, to use the Middle Ages' own word for poet. But in too many other passages of the major poetry, he is less successful, and becomes more of an unoriginal and awkward and tasteless revivalist than a genuine "maker." If *Arabia Deserta* can be compared to a more authentic and original "Royal Pavilion"—the building whose Eastern domes and spires contrast sharply with the usual architecture of England's Brighton—of English literature, then Doughty's major poetry must remind us of Victorian Gothic architecture, with the mixture of frequently tasteless failure and sudden, unexpected success that this comparison implies.

In the combination of a genuinely successful recreation of some Gothic (and in the case of *Adam Cast Forth*, Eastern) elements and a derivative ugliness, Doughty's poetry turns out to be very representative of its age rather than the unique throwback that its proponents (and Doughty himself) have claimed. And the intense debate over his poetic greatness or total lack of worth may be the result of the same qualities that make Victorian Gothic architecture difficult to defend artistically but occasionally pleasing to some minds nonetheless. A reasoned analysis of the structure, characterization, style, and philosophy of each poem will reveal Doughty's status as a minor, if worthy, poet very much of his period.

II   Dawn in Britain: *Intention and Plot*

Doughty thought this epic of seven hundred pages his major life-work (though *Mansoul* his best poem), and had it in mind as early as 1865 when he was still an undergraduate. By contrast, *Arabia Deserta* was for him only a digression. Finished in 1903, *Dawn* was composed over a period of approximately ten years, a testimony to Doughty's seriousness of intent.

As Doughty's postscript to the poem indicates, it, like *Arabia Deserta*, was to serve his purpose of reviving pre-Shakespearean English, and Doughty's preparation for his task included the same deep study of words and the taking of the thesauruslike "word notes" that characterize the composition of all his works. His research in history and literature was also arduous. He knew Homer's epic in Massero's Italian translation and read very deeply in history in the form of medieval and Renaissance chronicles like those of Holinshed and Geoffrey of Monmouth, read the Roman historians, and of course was familiar with the version of British history that appears in book 2, canto 10 of Spenser's *The Faerie Queene*. Thus, he includes all-but-forgotten corners of history, like the failed Roman attempt to take Yemen, Veronius's legend of Joseph of Arimithea, who is credited with introducing Christianity into Britain, and Druidic rites. He intended in *Dawn* nothing less than the immediate reliving of the shadowy 450 years from the conquest of Rome by Gallic tribes to the destruction of Jerusalem by Titus. He wanted not merely to imitate ancient epics but rather to write his own fresh, original epic of early Britain as if he were a Chaucerian-Spenserian poet, and to allow his reader to experience the grammar and therefore the thought of another time. However we may judge Doughty's success in this endeavor, its very scope must compel respect.

A look at the basic plot structure clarifies the nature and concerns of this long poem of myriad characters and historical events. The poem divides naturally into four sections, each of which contains the story of a major hero who embodies an important theme. Doughty does not organize the poem into four main sections; he divides it instead into twenty-four books, a more confusing because arbitrary method. Any given "book" could contain more or less action, or stop and start at a different point in the narrative than it does. If we simply follow the stories of each of the four heroes without paying attention to Doughty's book divisions, the narrative lines quickly fall into place, although they are obscured by a wealth of detail and digressive action in the poem itself.

Brennus, the British Gallic chieftain, who succeeds in conquering Rome, predominates in book 1 through the middle of book 5 and represents the barbarian virtues of martial prowess and spiritual forthrightness. In these opening books, we see how the British Isles are occupied by Gallic tribes and how Prince Brennus, son of Dunwallon, composes his quarrels with Duke Heremod and his own brother, Belinus. Brennus becomes king of his uncle Correus's domain, weds Heremod's sister Fridia, and goes on with Heremod to subdue Spain, make pacts with other Gallic tribes, and cross the Alps into Tuscany. The wave of conquest spreading from Britain eastward culminates in the capture of the city of Rome, toward which Brennus behaves generously. Under Brennus's grandson's nephew (Brennus having been ambushed and killed in the meanwhile), the second Brennus, Greece also falls to the Gauls. The suicide of the second Brennus, caused by the gods' revenge for his sacking of Phoebus's temple, ends the outward movement of the Gauls and this section of the poem. The city Senogallia, founded by first Brennus's Gauls on the Adriatic coast, remains a monument to Gallic power even during the period of Rome's strength and Gallic decline.

In book 6, the tide of martial and spiritual conquest begins to flow from East to West. A resurgent Rome attempts the conquest of Britain and fails, but Joseph of Arimithea, one of Christ's earliest disciples and the second main hero of the poem, sails from Palestine bringing the new religion, Christianity. After many adventures, including an attack on his vessel by all the powers of Hell, kindly reception by the Roman Priscus, and attack by superstitious continental Gauls, Joseph and his followers arrive in Britain and find refuge in King Duneda's Avalon despite the opposition of the chief Druid, Aesgar. Joseph represents love and kindness in contrast to the bloodshed and superstition of the pagan world, and we watch his doctrine begin to take root in Britain with increasing strength, through conversion and good works. This basic story takes us through the middle of book 10, but Joseph remains in the background of the rest of the poem until he and his doctrines assume dominance in the last book.

Caradoc or Caratacus, the protagonist to whom half the poem is dedicated, embodies the budding spirit of British nationalism and fortitude in the face of successful Roman invasion and remains with us from this point through book 21, reappearing briefly only to die at the end of book 24. We watch him develop (as Brennus and Joseph do not) as a personality, beginning with his unsuccessful efforts to avert war as his father's ambassador to Rome and his stereotypical rescue of and romance with Embla, Dumnoveros's daughter. He leads the British forces through the long and hopeless Roman wars in which he achieves maturity of leadership, only to be betrayed by the wicked northern harlot Queen Cartismandua. His final confrontation with Emperor Claudius as a captive in the Roman arena, pardon, retirement to the Gallic city of Senogallia, and witnessing of the burning of Rome during a civil war takes us back in memory to Brennus's capture of Rome.

The Roman gentleman Pudens, the last of Doughty's heroes, represents in his conversion to Christianity and marriage with the British convert Rosmerta (books 22–23), the synthesis between Roman sophistication, British bravery and directness, and Christian charity toward which the poem has been working since its beginning. In his struggle to accept the new faith we see the absorption of pagan and Roman elements into Christianity and the formation of a new British personality. In the final book (24), Doughty attempts to tie the knot of his four heroes' narrative threads by chronicling the death of the old world—symbolized by the destruction of the last Druidic temples, the conquest of Jerusalem by Titus, and the self-destruction of Rome as witnessed by the dying King Caradoc—and the birth of the new, seen in Pudens's and Rosmerta's Christian life and Joseph's final vision of Rome's adoption of Christianity. The misty origin of Britain—the "Utmost Isle" in Doughty's original title of his poem—with its incessant tribal warfare and Druidic religion, has given way in Doughty's vision to the dawn of a new, civilized nation, Christian and self-consciously patriotic.

A host of minor personalities and events fills out the large contours of Doughty's epic, sometimes overwhelming it. The most prominent minor stories remain those of Togodumnos, Caradoc's brother, and Thorolf, his Germanic ally, both staunch warriors; Fridia, Brennus's wife and Embla, Caradoc's wife, fit companions for their noble husbands; the evil Cartismandua; Claudius, weak Roman emperor; and Cuan, the British Christian bard who sees Jesus as "our Druid." Two love interludes, the Crispin-Agygia/Cusmon-Verica and Cloten-Esla tales, add necessary relief to a poem composed largely of battles and warriors.

III   Dawn in Britain: *Structure*

Even this synopsis—which of necessity omits many minor incidents and personalities—raises an immediate question about the structure of the poem: can so vast a work, uniting Rome, Roman Palestine, and Britain over 450 years and including a cast of hundreds, if not thousands, be unified? Barker Fairley, the most convinced exponent of the poem's unity, paraphrases Doughty's *Mansoul* cathedral-poem metaphor in stating that "The poem is grandly planned, the site is well considered, the pattern of the place is plotted out with the utmost care."[2] But Middleton Murry calls *Dawn* "a long, vague, intricate story which" Doughty "who had little or no architectonic gift, could not conrol."[3]

If we consider this question objectively, we find that fully half the epic—the five Brennus books, seven or eight of the Caradoc books, and the Boudicca revolt against Rome of the last books—concerns warfare. Spiritually, Doughty's relish for depicting battles begins to transform what is supposed to be a poem about Christian love into a Shaw Brothers' Kung Fu film in verse. Structurally, the excess of warfare—where two or three major battles would have done as well—causes the inclusion of many kings, lords, and warriors who are little more than shadow figures. The reader begins to lose track of these with alarming frequency: who remembers, or can remember, King Kynan and Lord Hiradoc, or any of the minor Gallic chieftains, or even the more defined Roman generals, outside of Claudius himself?

More seriously, Doughty's larger themes get lost in a swirl of myriad, small, repetitive, digressive actions. The poet's habit of beginning new plots—such as the introduction of the Christians in book 6 and Caratacus's Roman journey in book 10—in the middle of books, rather than at their beginning or end, further causes the reader to miss their full significance. Important events like Caradoc's rage over Thorolf's death are placed so that they are submerged in the flow of less important events, as book 19's "Argument" clearly reveals. Fairley defends this characteristic of Doughty's by calling it a replica of medieval "cumulative" development in which major events are purposely not highlighted. It may be medieval, or it may be a "bad accident," as T. E. Lawrence once put it. In either case, it is not good: the whole epic suffers from a lack of clear definition of important as opposed to unimportant events, the result of indiscriminate overcrowding, much in the manner of Victorian Gothic architectural facades.

The last book, in which Doughty has left himself the important and nearly impossible job of pulling his huge skein together, remains an example of his poor structural judgment. Instead of concentrating on Pudens and Rosmerta, Joseph and Caradoc only, he chooses to introduce the apostle Simon, a new character who appeared only toward the end of book 23, and his wanderings. Rosmerta, now called Claudia after her conversion, appears only in the form of dead "letters," after having been made much of in the last two books. Phelles's martyr's death at the hands of a few remaining Druids, Cuan's contest with the pagan bard Talaith and his visit to King Duneda's court, and Agricola's destruction of Mona all take precedence over Caradoc's death, which is handled in relatively few, abrupt lines. Jerusalem's conquest by Titus happens suddenly and is complete in five lines; Joseph's death is made too obviously to coincide with the end of the book and follows too abruptly on the scene in Duneda's court.

We understand that Doughty wanted the Christian theme to predominate and to kill off the old pagan world, but he has too much to handle in one book, and Caradoc's character is completely swamped by the mass of detail. Doughty's attempt to paint a panoramic ending of diverse shifting scenes leaves us with skeleton actions but no feeling of conviction about them. Fairley is right that Doughty has a basic plan and resolves the action of the epic, but more important, unfortunately, is the fact that Doughty's inability to proportion and highlight obscures and robs his intellectually worked out structure of the power and logic that it should have.

In *Arabia Deserta,* Doughty's meandering structure copies the actual wanderings of a real-life journey, and the mixture of scientific digression, incident, tales, and reflection charms us as the portrait of a nervous, inquiring mind at work on a new, uncertain situation. As T. E. Lawrence comments in his introduction to the book, Doughty's sudden shifts of subject actually reproduce the feverish reactions of travelers in the desert. In a work of fiction, we demand a much smoother structure, in which every detail contributes directly to the point of the whole. But Doughty's poem could have been cut by half and the major characters far better highlighted.

IV   Dawn in Britain: *Characterization*

John Holloway compares the characterization in *Arabia Deserta* with that in *Dawn* as follows:

Middleton Murry exaggerated in saying, as he once did, that only what Doughty wrote about Arabia remained alive; but it may be true that he was at his best when he could draw either directly, or indirectly, on his Arabian experiences. There, he had actually seen primitive men and women: the men often noble and gentle, but at the same time erratic and vengeful and fanatical. . . . Maybe Doughty would have thought it unpatriotic to represent early British heroes in this mixed light. At all events he makes them much more conventionally heroic figures; and he pays the price.[4]

If Doughty's epic, despite its frequently interesting and powerful stylistic experimentation, strikes us rather like an overlong "B" grade Cecil B. DeMille "spectacular" film, complete with descending hordes, much blood, simpleminded romantic scenes, and equally simpleminded underlying patriotic and moralistic assumptions, its one-dimensional and not-too-bright "noble" and "wicked" characters are at least as responsible as any other element in its literary texture. Intelligence and complexity are the two important qualities lacking in all Doughty's characters in *Dawn*, including the major stars. Except for Caradoc, no one develops beyond the gray hair involved in getting old, and even Caradoc is too good, too pure, and too simple for this world. In Chaucer (and in *Arabia Deserta*), each of the pilgrims has his faults; Gawain fails the moral test in *Gawain and the Green Knight*, thus learning that mortals are imperfect and in need of God's grace; and Spenser's Red Crosse Knight has far from an easy road to spiritual triumph.

Doughty's British heroes, on the other hand, exhibit unwavering perfection from the start, while his non-Christian Romans and Jews are almost inevitably cowardly and motivated by base thoughts. His portrayal of Jews as "Christ slaying"[5] and "false"[6] reveals the same prejudiced thinking that appears in the intolerant narrator's voice in *Arabia Deserta* and argues very strongly against Fairley's and John Heath-Stubbs' claims for the poem's "universality."[7] Unlike *Arabia Deserta*, the poem lacks totally the characters who would argue against Doughty's prejudices, thus modifying them. Doughty's characters in *Dawn* inhabit the world of the comic book, complete with noble superhuman heroes and dastardly villains. If Doughty had done this tongue in cheek, like Tolkien, we might enjoy it; but he is unremittingly serious and unsophisticated in believing Britons and their allies—aside from an occasional wicked traitor—"good," and others—aside from one philo-Semitic kind Jew and a Roman or two—"bad." If, like

Tolkien, he had written total fantasy and forgotten about actual history, he could have gotten away with "good" and "bad" characters. But his insistence on basing everything on real history opens him to the charge of partisanship.

His major characters become interchangeable and unreal. Brennus's Fridia and Caradoc's Embla might have been the victims of wife-swapping without anyone's knowing it: both are equally brave and "good." On page 94, he uses the word "Gauls" eleven times without ever varying or adding color to the people so described. Brennus is continually portrayed as "godlike Brennus" and loses his humanity as a result, as even Fairley agrees. Their fainting mother Corwenna reconciles Belin and Brennus in a melodramatic scene barely worthy of a soap opera: "She, furious, beats, alas! / Her royal breast" (*Dawn*, 33). The epic tone adds a touch of the ludicrous to the false action. Since melodrama consists of one part sickly sentimentality and one part sensationally cruel violence, we are not surprised to find Brennus participating in just such actions and no others.

Joseph of Arimithea should express the complex inner life of an early Christian but unfortunately displays only another facet of Doughty's inherent poetic sentimentality instead of an Augustine-like subtlety. From the first a "just man and honourable councillor" (*Dawn*, 167), his role never varies in the course of hundreds of pages. Always ready to help others and to pray for the good of humanity (especially when it converts to his creed), Joseph lacks even one of the natural human weaknesses that make Christianity a necessary and appealing religion in the first place, and which could have made his embodiment of its values graphically meaningful instead of simply asserted. He even dies kneeling in prayer. When Joseph faith-heals Rosmerta, Prince Kowain's daughter and later a convert herself (*Dawn*, 230), Doughty appears to have forgotten his own faith in Western science rather than superstition. Because he lacks complexity and interest, we suffer Joseph rather than believe with him, and he remains memorable only in a sentimental, slightly ludicrous sense.

Caradoc or Caratacus remains Doughty's major hero since half the poem stands on his broad shoulders. Here Doughty's Gothic "cumulative" method of redundancy and familiarity through long exposure has some effect as we watch Caradoc develop from an inexperienced young man to a care-worn leader and a weary old man over the course of many books. But essentially he plays only the almost unchangeably bright side of a coin whose opposite is the tarnished Roman Emperor

Claudius, who is invariably "impotent" and cowardly in Doughty's depiction.

As he rescues Embla from ruffians in a clichéd scene, shows unstinting bravery in battle, and falls victim to Cartismandua's dastardly treachery, we realize that all Doughty's descriptions of him are mere variants of the line "Swells the great heart of noble Caradoc" (*Dawn*, 307). While Roman armies suffer sedition and Roman imperialism is always grasping and base, Caradoc's, like Brennus's, imperial motives are inevitably noble, like his love for Embla, and his actions entirely predictable.

Most of all, we rarely read Caradoc's inner thoughts. When Doughty grants us a glimpse of these, his hero becomes human for brief moments. Caradoc's grief over Thorolf's death, his appearance before Claudius in Rome, and his death are memorable events. The death of Thorolf, Caradoc's Germanic ally, takes place in book 19. As usual Doughty fails to set off this death and places it in the middle rather than at the beginning or end of the book, with the result that it is less powerful than it might have been. Thorolf in any case is not well realized: we are told that "Thorolf is, in force, / As a wild bull" (*Dawn*, 308), and not much more remains of him. Although we cannot feel Caradoc's grief for him because Thorolf has never come alive in the first place, the grief itself, with Caradoc wildly striking trees in the forest, is well portrayed and gives a tangible sense of loneliness in the face of death: "He is alone, with Death, in this dark wood" (*Dawn*, 527).

The picture of a conquered Caradoc appearing before Claudius in Rome is also well imagined, and here Doughty begins the book with Caradoc's speech. His lines

> "Romans! whilst I viewed, from hence,
> Your palaces, your gilded temple-roofs,
> I MARVELLED, YE COULD COVET OUR POOR COTES!"
>   (*Dawn*, 578)

go to the heart of the folly of late nineteenth-century British no less than Roman imperialism, although Doughty never realizes this connection anywhere in his poetic work or thought. He even praises the British "safety" or concentration camps invented in the Boer War in *The Cliffs*[8] through the mouth of the German Lieutenant Weise! And at least one contemporary reviewer[9] noticed the close connection between *Dawn in Britain* and the mindlessly jingoistic *Under Arms,* which argues in favor of the Boer War and was written during the same period as *Dawn.* Commenting on Doughty's simple patriotism, T. E. Lawrence wrote in 1923 that "A bigger man would not read the *Morning Post.*"[10] But although Doughty as poet never acts on Caradoc's insight, in this scene for a change we see rather than hear about Caradoc's ability to think. Although Caradoc's death is unfortunately subordinated to all the other action of the final book 24, and is too brief a moment, his final dream of a British funeral for Togodumnos his brother is touching as he relives in his imagination scenes from his own life against a background of burning Rome (*Dawn*, 681). Here, as in the other two scenes mentioned above, we see something of an inner self. But in thirty thousand lines we have too few moments like these.

Pudens and Rosmerta, who should be heroes of thought, suffer from a stale idealistic conventionality. Pudens's conversion to Christianity lacks a deep motive: "She loveth him, for Christ; he Christ, for her" (*Dawn*, 634). Doughty realizes this, because he gives Pudens some last sad musings about the old Roman gods of his youth and makes him wait until his conversion is felt before allowing him to marry Rosmerta; but it is all too thin and pat. And Rosmerta's personality suffers from the same goody-goody lack of human stain that plagues Joseph's:

> Briton Rosmerta, Roman spouse, so bears,
> These days, her meekly, in her new estate;
> That all her love, which look upon her face.
> (*Dawn*, 644)

An inversion cannot make a thought like "That all her love, which look upon her face" original. Instead of an authentic insight into the mind of early Christianity, we have here the dull, grey, and conventional facade of a nineteenth-century Salvation Army building. We do not see Doughty's characters in *Dawn* as living human beings, and cannot easily relate to their simple thoughts, except in rare moments. With its weak structure, the main failing of this poem is that we cannot empathize with or believe in its heroes.

V   Dawn in Britain: *Style*

Middleton Murry writes about the style of *Dawn* that Doughty "became not merely archaistic, but insensitive and tyrannous. With a kind of frenzied implacability he would torture English syntax and compel words to do his bidding."[11] But John Heath-Stubbs finds that "The peculiar archaic, yet terse and economical language, which he fashioned for himself, has itself a primitive quality and an essential dignity, fitted to its material."[12] Who is right?

We will understand what Doughty wanted to do in his creation of *Dawn*'s neo-epic style if we look at a book which he in all probability did not read, but which had immense influence on his period. In Ruskin's *Stones of Venice*, which appeared in 1853 and argued for a revival of the Gothic spirit in English architecture, we find a catalog of six "moral elements" of Gothic:

1. Savageness
2. Changefulness
3. Naturalism
4. Grotesqueness
5. Rigidity
6. Redundance[13]

We find precisely these elements in Doughty's poem. By "Savageness" Ruskin means the "rude and wild"[14] nature of northern art, which Doughty attempts to capture in his rough, lumbering movement of heavy punctuation and inversion and realistic portrayals of battles and suffering; "Changefulness" indicates the lack of concern with symmetry and use of detail at the expense of a smooth finish that we see in the digressions and profusion of detail, sometimes to the detriment of clear basic structure, of almost all Doughty's poetry; "Naturalism," or "the love of natural objects for their own sake, and the effort to represent them frankly, unconstrained by artistical laws,"[15] appears in Doughty's concrete, unmetaphorical adherence to natural objects themselves; "Grotesqueness," or "the tendency to delight in the fantastic and ludicrous, as well as in sublime, images,"[16] results in the many hellish monsters that attack the Christians' vessel in book 7 of *Dawn*; "Rigidity," or "an elastic tension and communication of force from part to part" which errs "if at all, ever on the side of brusquerie,"[17] is seen in Doughty's jerky, abrupt syntax; and "Redundancy," or "the accumulation of ornament," we see constantly in what Fairley calls Doughty's medieval "cumulative" method of building up characters and effects by piling on detail over long stretches of his poems, *Dawn* in particular.

As the style of *Dawn in Britain* itself reveals, Doughty intended to revive these very qualities in a new epic. The answer to the critical controversy over style delineated in the beginning of this section lies in our judgment of his success in attaining his goals. If we take a passage like

> Her spouse, she loves: and Pudens if her, maid,
> He, erewhile, loved all earthly thing above,
> Much more her now he loves. . . .
>
> (*Dawn*, 644)

we see the heavy inversions and use of punctuation caused by Doughty's deliberately "savage" and "rigid" (to use Ruskin's terms) style. And we also see that "And Pudens if her, maid, / He, erewhile" is devastatingly awkward and ugly for conveying the simple thought that Pudens now loves Rosmerta more than ever.

Similarly, the lines

> When silent, captive, lies, at afternoon,
> The city; wander Gauls in Roman streets,
> By companies, and in houses and in halls,
> They enter; and thence, wondering, draw forth preys,
> Which, heaped in open places, to Gauls' gods,
> Much precious stuff, will they, by fire, consume.
>
> (*Dawn*, 102)

appear unnecessarily clotted and stumbling for the expression of what is mere recitative, or passages which serve as plot connections. In both passages, the reader feels that Doughty has no *reason* to twist syntax, and that he is doing it only for the simple reason of being different. The result is a feeling of contrived ugliness that serves no particular purpose. In these passages, and very, very many more like them, we see the "fanatic" Doughty who applies a theory of language and style like a straitjacket over content whether it will go or not, whether it is justified or not. As Middleton Murry claims, the desire to forge a new epic style has resulted in simple ugliness here. And the very frequent use of such clichéd poeticisms as "lo" and "doth" only adds to the feeling that we are witnessing in many passages a derivative, awkward, and stale Gothic revival rather than a fresh new kind of Gothic or a genuine insight into the past.

But fortunately for the poem, this is not the whole story. In a passage like the following, which details Caradoc's primitive rationalization of death and is also singled out for praise by Heath-Stubbs, the gnarled slow quality of the style speaks to us like the powerfully harsh strokes of a Durer woodcut:

> But who lie, gaping upright, in the grave,
> Whose rottenness we rue; ben not their deaths,
> (Night-sleep, this iron griesly grip, which hath
> None wakening, clod laid under clodded earth,)
> Surcease of burdens, and of every pain,
> Less grievous than our life, which yet, the sun
> See'th; that, like sháft's flight, tossed in every blast;
> Whereon, again, the woundless air doth close:
> Or like as tainted footstep, in this snow,
> Soon fading; which wherewith, doth utterly perish!
> But, and when cometh aught thing, of good, to us,
> Is that a seldom grace! King Caradoc felt
> His heart, like a burning coal, in his cold breast,
> For Thorolf's death, his brother, in Mainland.
>   (*Dawn*, 526)

We have the heavy use of punctuation and inversions, combined with archaic words, that we have in less successful passages. But here the situation—Thorolf's death and Caradoc's loneliness—and the meditation involved justify this style. Doughty's vaguely Shakespearean metaphors of the arrow and the fading footstep suit the atmosphere perfectly. The alliterations fall on important words—"whose rottenness we rue," "griesly grip"—and not just anywhere, as in the line "A light Dumnonian keel, of King Duneda" (*Dawn*, 332), for instance, which strikes us as an alliteration for alliteration's sake. "Night-sleep, this iron griesly grip" could scarcely be more chillingly concrete. The inverted emphasis on "his brother" in "For Thorolf's death, his brother, in Mainland" is strangely affecting where "For Thorolf his brother's death in Mainland" would have been smoothly derivative and without impact. "Mainland" strikes us as an entirely appropriate term for pre-Europe, and it is difficult to think of a better one. When Doughty has something to say with it, and his devices can be related to precise reasons and effects rather than the general desire to create "a" style, his style convinces as do few others.

The poem contains many surprising successes along with ludicrous failures. This brief descriptive passage remains memorable for its incredible combination of heavy Gothic *w* and gracefully light Spenserian *s* sounds. The Mediterranean becomes a Norwegian glacier lake while retaining a light charm:

> Tyre's large sand shore, like sickle, lies beyond;
> That strewed is, after Winter's stormy wrath,
> With shells and shining wealth of salt sea-deep:
> Whose world of billows, like to watery light,
> Melodious, had lulled his cradle-sleep.
>
> (*Dawn*, 674)

It is as if Doughty challenges himself to achieve delicacy and grace despite the hard sounds of his chosen vocabulary and *w* alliterations, and emerges victorious against all odds. He refuses to go the smooth and sweet way, and the result in the good passages is a unique kind of heavier Chaucerian utterance which captures the atmosphere of the cold, harsh north.

The reader continually comes upon genuinely poetic perceptions rendered in Doughty's surprising style. We remember the bowstring characterized as a "humming nerve," the "bitter fork-head" of an arrow, the "blue-ribbed ice" of a northern lake, the "sheen sharp heads" of spears, the "magic chant borne on the wavering wind" of Druidic rites. For a few brief moments, we move in a simpler, fresher, and more sensory world than our own. We do not easily forget the Roman and pagan funerals, Druidic chants, Cuan's bardic songs, and the meals in Brennus's and Caradoc's great halls. In a constrained, abrupt, harsh style which rules out normal diction, syntax, and rhythms—and perhaps subtlety of meditative thought as well— Doughty has rendered more lines well than anyone could have guessed. Heath-Stubbs simply forgets about all the passages in which the style does not work, while Murry sees none of those where it does. A comment made about Melville's long poem *Clarel* by Walter Bezanson brings us surprisingly close to the stylistic success and failure of *Dawn in Britain* (and *Mansoul*) as well:

One feels a poet who sensed the violence with which at times language must be ripped and cut and jammed into place, but who was not always able, like the good poet, to make one feel the rightness of the result. If one margin of the verse is softened by the worn-out language of the contemporary genteel tradition, the opposite margin is hardened by hardness. . . . At the successful center there is a curious mixture of the archaic and the contemporary both in language and in materials. Melville may well have had some notion that his ancient setting justified, even called for, a measure of antiquarianism.[18]

Too often, Doughty's style exists for its own sake without finding a close companion in its content, and substitutes harsh awkwardness or poetic cliché for fresh perception; but in its moments of success, we feel that he has discovered a way of making the past come alive. As Samuel Chew puts it in a statement about all of Doughty's poetry, "Those who force their way into his fastness will discover flowers of poetry growing amid the rocks."[19] Although we cannot call *Dawn in Britain* on the whole a successful or even an enjoyably readable poem, its obstinate attempt to get back to the roots of Doughty's own civilization is part of the same quest that sent him into Arabia; and his unevenly workable epic style is one of the search's most interesting fruits. No poet will have to explore that territory again.

VI   Adam Cast Forth: *Introduction and Synopsis*

Murry praises *Adam Cast Forth: A Sacred Drama in Five Songs* (1908) as a "great" poem despite his condemnation of *Dawn* as practically worthless. T. E. Lawrence liked it most among Doughty's poems, and Anne Treneer writes that "Anyone who writes about Doughty must feel a little loathe to leave *Adam Cast Forth:* it is the poem in which the virtue that was in him is least impeded by his wilfulness in twisting the natural word-order of English, which was his poetic bane."[20] *Adam* was begun early in 1907 and first titled *Hawwa;* it had been on Doughty's mind for twenty years and he had first hoped to use its Arabian theme as the first canto of an epic. Perhaps fortunately, *Dawn* satisfied Doughty's epic ambitions, for he chose a more simple style when he finally sat down to write this brief Arabian "drama" four years after *Dawn* was completed.

In addition to a less "elevated" or pompous tone than *Dawn's*, *Adam Cast Forth's* lyricism makes itself felt in a more easy, streamlined style which, while retaining Doughty's characteristic archaisms and inversions, is pared down to an ultimate simplicity. The poem uses more Arabic—and for the first time Hebrew—words than any of the other poems, and thus reminds us of *Arabia Deserta*. The patriotic and partisan Victorian Christian imperialist disappears completely, and a deeper, more universal mind, partaking of Semitic bareness and time-lessness, takes his place. The poet's deep sweetness and gentleness—tapped only in *Arabia Deserta* and parts of *Mansoul* among the other works—appear in a compact drama that focuses on two major characters.

Instead of a garish and unsuccessful Gothic Revival cathedral like *Dawn*, Doughty in this poem has created a small, pre-Christian chapel, nicely proportioned and relatively austere, which harks back to another age without appearing derivative or a conscious recreation. Despite a few remaining Victorianisms of thought and form, it manages to achieve an Adamic freshness that nineteenth-century American writers also concerned with this approach might have found interesting.

Basically, Doughty expands Gen. 3:16–24, which relates Adam and Eve's punishment, into a whole poem, whose purpose is to explain how Adam and Eve developed from godlike, mythical—and nonhuman—creatures into real human beings, the founders of the human race as we know it today. Doughty is interested in what happened to the couple *after* they were cast out of Eden, just as he found himself in exile in Arabia. He prefaces his "Sacred Drama in Five Songs" with a "Judaeo-Arabian Legend": "Adam and Hawwa, cast forth from the PARADISE, fell down in several places of the Earth: whence they, after age-long wandering, meet together again, upon a Mountain."[21]

"The First Song" opens with a monologue by Sammael, or Satan, who accuses God of injustice. According to Sammael, God created Adam out of pride, so Adam could praise him, but botched the job, making Adam a combination of spirit and "base ferment of beast's flesh" (4), easy to deceive. Yet God blames Adam for the Fall, and has punished him and Adama, or Eve, for one hundred years, during which they wandered a harsh, dry, and wind-blown earth as exiles from Eden. Now the punishment appears to be over as Sammael notes God's angel going down to see suffering Adam.

Ezriel, God's angel, informs an old, blind, and broken Adam that Adama, from whom he had become separated, will be restored to him and that he and she will multiply. An Adama (Hebrew for "Earth"), who has lost her power of speech, is reunited with blind Adam. As he feels her face and she attempts to speak to him, the reader feels a power of touch deeper than words in this poem.

In "The Second Song," the pair grow accustomed to their new state. They see death in the form of a dead camel—a very Arabic motif—

and this reminds them of their fallen condition. They remember the Garden of Eden as an idyllic past world where they were innocent with the perceptions of children. As they regain their former strength, they relate stories of their expulsion and respective wanderings until the appearance of Ezriel. Adam, in contrast to the rebellious Sammael, has learned during the hundred years of suffering to accept God's judgments: "We may not question with the Lord, nor ask, / Why dost THOU thus? nor gainsay, in our hearts" (40). They sleep in the Bunyanesque "Valley of the Lord's Rest," where Ezriel has sent them.

"The Third Song" contrasts the pair's exposure to rain and mist for the first time, with a two-day trek through a desolate area very reminiscent of the Arabian desert: "We breathe a flame; we tread on glowing rocks; / How may we endure, until day's ending thus?" (50–51). They face the fury of Satan's powers, but are rescued by angels. Adam again remembers the Garden of Eden and how he taught Adama and loved her: "I looking, in thine eyes, thee O Adama I loved! / That gazed so inwardly on mine" (65). The song closes on this happy note as memories preserve the couple in their present hard test of obedience decreed by God.

"The Fourth Song" tells of Adam's illness and Adama's devotion to him. He revives on the fifth day after their reunion and struggles onward to the goal of final restfulness offered by God through his angels; "thick wárm salt living blood" (74) shoots from his nostrils as evidence of his exertion. When they arrive near the promised destination, he must learn to dig in order to drink. Ezriel grants Adam a vision of the future, including wars and the Flood, but he also shows him a simple wedding. In singling out this particular custom as a balance for the destructive side of man's nature, Doughty indicates the high value he places on male-female relations. Adam never blames Adama for the Fall, and Doughty calls the pair "The Adam" sometimes, indicating their oneness. God refuses to do away with death, as Adam asks him to, but Doughty indicates that marriage and reproduction are an answer to this dreaded force.

The final song finds the pair in another Bunyanesque setting, the "Valley of Vision." "Earth's Field," the promised destination of peace and fertility, is revealed to them. "I will enable you," (95) says God, to do the work necessary for survival, and we remember the Arabs' use of the word "enable" in *Arabia Deserta* to mean "make potent." They learn about the ocean, its fishes, and the seasons. "The World" begins, as the chorus informs us (110), when Adama gets pregnant. As she gives birth in pain to Kayin, Habel (Cain and Abel), and a daughter, Noaba, her name becomes Hawwa, Arabic for "being." The song and the poem close as the new human family, having learned to till "Earth's Field" and make fire, huddles in a warm, secure, womblike cave while a cold winter rages outside.

VII   Adam Cast Forth: *Theme*

Doughty has written a loose lyric "drama" without the usual obvious dramatic tension of opposed forces. Sammael disappears early in the piece and influences no decisions: after one hundred years of torment for disobedience, Adam has learned to accept the fate God decrees. We are told about rather than shown the pair's hundred years of suffering, when "Sarsar," God's siroccolike wind, blew them about. (Any reader who has experienced a Near Eastern "khamsin" or Southern California "Santa Ana" for just a few days will appreciate the extremity of Adam and Adama's punishment by God without being shown the details.) Ezriel tells us early in the poem that God has ordained the successful conclusion of their struggle, and we are in little doubt that he is right. How then—in the apparent absence of tension and suspense—does Doughty manage to achieve the compressed impact that marks this poem?

By simplifying his story, Doughty forces us to focus totally on the developing minds of Adam and Adama and the allegorical physical struggle that accompanies this development. Without distractions, we watch Adam and Adama undergo a painful transformation from creatures who, though chastised, remain sensual and childlike to logical, self-conscious, and limited but recognizably human beings. Doughty captures a process of alteration of consciousness. This is the struggle: God's anger and harsh mercy actually temper and refine man into human form.

In terms of Adama's name, she goes from the dustlike state that Sammael says is half of man's nature, and which is implied by her name ("earth" in Hebrew) to the "being" or consciousness which is the meaning of her second name, Hawwa. Doughty actually chronicles the Fall of humanity from superhuman to human but presents this as a blessing in disguise. Suffering enables man to find the godlike qualities of faith and fortitude in himself and to appreciate the Edenic qualities of our world. In this view, Doughty accepts a variation on the doctrine of the Fortunate Fall, which holds that without the Fall man would not have experienced the joy of the Redeemer, or Jesus. Doughty's vision, as expressed through the drama of *Adam Cast Forth,* is remarkably similar to the intellectual approach of Henry James's father, who—as R. W. B. Lewis has pointed out—in his *Christianity the Logic of Creation* (1857) had argued that "'Adam's fall,' as it is called, was not that stupid lapse from the divine favor which it has vulgarly been reputed to have been, but an actual rise to the normal human level."

Sammael presents God as having created man with inherent weaknesses and then punishing him for acting weakly. Doughty's poem attempts to answer this charge—thus "justifying the ways of God to men" in Milton's words—by revealing that Adam's new state, although not the blissful ease of Eden, includes the greater quality of hard-won love and appreciation that Adam and Adama could never have felt for one another and the land in their comfortable Edenic state. Thus God seems harsh but is actually beneficent. We follow the hard proof of this proposition through the pair's changing perceptions with subtle interest.

VIII   Adam Cast Forth: *Perceptions and Language*

Doughty reveals the change in man's consciousness by displaying a remarkable ability to see things through the early Adam's eyes. Death, rain, and fish are new things to be viewed with gaping wonder as Doughty cuts through the accretions of his own personality and gives us not the Victorian geologist of *Arabia Deserta,* so eager to classify and measure, but the inner Adamic poet who presents the world in a new light. Doughty's deepest "thoughts" were sensory perceptions and feelings going beyond words. Only in this poem does he manage like a Beduin *kassâd,* or poet, to express this, totally subordinating the rational intellect, and reaching back to the most primitive state where seeing is being. "Had feeling every sense" (29), says an Adam concerned with seeing, hearing, smelling, and feeling until near the end of the poem when as an agriculturalist he begins to experience the rudiments of more abstract intellectual qualities.

The freshness of Adam and Adama's perceptions appear in the relatively large number of Hebrew words used in this one poem. As we saw in the discussion of *Arabia Deserta*'s biblical influences, Doughty began learning Hebrew in 1906, possibly in order to use it in *Adam Cast Forth,* which he had begun to think about. The evidence of his copy of the Hebrew Bible and a small portion of Genesis in his King James Bible now in the Gonville and Caius Library tell us that he learned only nouns and had a very basic, almost nonexistent knowledge of the Hebrew verb system. But in *Adam Cast Forth* he has put his imperfect knowledge of Hebrew to good use, beginning with the names of his two major characters.

"Adam" means "man" in Hebrew, and contains the roots of "blood," "red," and "earth" as well. Doughty takes the name to mean "red loam" (11), indicating that he is fully aware of the Hebrew implications. "Adamu," Adama's personal name for him, suggests a grammatical form of literary Arabic, in which the subject of a sentence takes "u" or "un." In *Arabia Deserta* we read that "*Edom*" actually means "the red" or "*ed dumm*" in Arabic (I, 46), and this name is also related to Adam and shows the close relationship between Arabic and Hebrew that Doughty recognized. "Adama," as stated in the plot synopsis, actually means "earth." "Hawwa" (Arabic), or "Chava" (Hebrew), or "Eve" (English), means "being," and is related to Doughty's translation of the tetragrammaton, God's name, as "I-AM," indicating her God-like ability to reproduce. Adam and Adama then are closely tied to the land and take on real "being" or existence only when they, like it, become fertile.

In *Adam Cast Forth,* we find many Hebrew words: "Harisuth" ("destruction"), "Satan" ("adversary"), "Bohu" ("emptiness," from the "tohu vavohu" of Genesis), "Ezriel" ("Helper of God"), "Cherub" (heavenly being close to angels), "liban" ("whiteness," used to signify sour milk), "Tehom" (the "Mother Deep" in Doughty's translation), and "Elyon" ("Most High"). God is "I-AM," Doughty's direct translation of the Hebrew letters YHWH. And there are more. Doughty sees our only approach to God as through words, and the older and more authentically tied to an oral, pre-script religious experience the better. Thus God is a "VOICE" and Adam at first recognizes Adama's voice although he cannot see her, and the whole poem is a dialogue to be spoken or read aloud. More specifically, we notice that Doughty employs the Hebrew language to describe the greatest mysteries, much in the manner of some ultraorthodox Jews who will not use it for anything but prayer. The highest, the lowest, utter chaos, good and evil, being, angels, God, all are expressed in Hebrew or sometimes Arabic rather than English. Doughty may well have come to feel the English of any period inadequate for the task of recording his deepest religious experiences.

In his personal King James Bible in the Gonville and Caius Library,
he marked Gen. 3:23, "Therefore the LORD God sent him forth from
the Garden of Eden, to till the ground from whence he was taken" and
his capitalization of "LORD" in this drama follows this translation. But
the old Hebrew words in themselves contain for Doughty an atmosphere of the past that English and English biblical translations alone
could not conjure up. If *Arabia Deserta* is an Anglo-Arabic work with
heavy biblical parallelisms and overtones, *Adam Cast Forth* is
Doughty's most biblical poem. In its monotonic, bare style it recalls
Jewish cantorial music or the music of Arabic songs. Although the narrator of *Arabia Deserta* finds Beduin music "monotonous," its influence obviously lingered. The straightforward lines with their alliterations remind us of the plainness of a religious chant:

> Under thy shoulders, so mine hands I set:
> Tread with me, and I with thine will match my steps.
> And when Beloved thou shalt be weary thus;
> Twine thou thine other arm, about my neck.
>   (*Adam*, 54)

The lines move naturally, the inversions are moderate, and there is no
artificial wrenching and juggling of sentence elements from their usual
places. In content, we have the simple variation on a single theme that
characterizes Near Eastern music. We also notice the biblical parallelism, the balancing of line against line and half line against half line
that Annette McCormick has shown is present in *Arabia Deserta* to a
great degree as well. When we add Adam's fatalistic acceptance of
God's word as transcending humanly perceivable justice, the case for
the biblical influence on this drama is complete, especially if we note
that Doughty has followed Gen. 3:16–24 at least as much as his
"Judaeo-Arabic fable" for his plot.

We also find many of the same old English words Doughty favored
in *Dawn in Britain;* these are his rough English equivalent to Hebrew
antiquity. However, the English words are used exclusively for the creation of a tactile Adamic first-time atmosphere, and relate to things
and actions known rather than to mysteries: rinded, chiddering, glis-
tering, derne, maunds, swonken, glebe, knapped, halm. Through the
combination of deeply echoing Hebrew words and more abruptly sensual English ones, Doughty attempts to capture the grammar of
thought and feeling of Adam himself.

Since Doughty's Adam-style is good for rendering sensory experience because of its simplicity as well as its old words, the Edenic memories of the pair are especially poignant. Doughty renders only memories of the Garden because he wants to show that "you can't go home again" as it were; Eden is past and done with and exists in the individual and the race only in deep memories. In a clear reference to the Song of Songs, Adam remembers how "When I awaking saw thee O Adama like / Hewed to fair blossom, in thy living flesh; / Thine eyes as Stars; and sunbright thy long locks; / And like sweet-smelling fruits, was the life's breath, / Of thy warm lips; ... / ... O what a joy was it, / To look in the LORD'S GARDEN, on my like. / And with a kindling ray of arcane love, / On mine, thy wandering pupils looked again" (63). But in Adam's comparison of Adama to the few things he knows—blossoms, stars, fruits—we realize that we are not reading about first love in the conventional sense or the sophisticated love of the Song of Songs, but rather are witnessing the *first love* ever, an "arcane" or deeply novel event.

Adama's memory of her first view of herself in the water of Eden also has a sensual, first-time quality apparent in its simply archaic style as well as the disarmingly gentle narcissism of its content:

> Therein I saw then, like an heavenly vision,
> Some Being more even than árt thou O Adamu fair!...
> I laughed, I spake: she laughed then, but not spake.
> And in her other hand, were fruits as these,
> And flowers like unto mine. Surprised mine heart,
> I startling leapt; and plashed therein my foot.
>
> (25)

The delicate parallelisms ("I laughed, I spake: she laughed then, but not spake") create a pleasing, halting feeling that captures Adama's childishly cautious approach to her own first-time experience of her reflection.

But after the Fall, the earth holds a more bitter novelty which Doughty's style captures sensuously in a passage like the following: "Father, I now thirsting stoopt, / To sup: but O, how bitter in my throat / This bíllow is!" (101). The discovery of salt water, captured in the contrast between the hard "bitter" and the softer Spenserian "billow," comes as an unwelcome surprise to Adama. Similarly, for Adama death is new and startling, and rendered as starkly as possible: "My

camel is and is not! / Fowl we knew not, / Fret, with crude bloody
beaks, ah her cold flesh!" (22).

The contrast between memories of the lost world and the harsh reality of the new one continually tortures the pair:

> Where, like as sheep, in hour of midday heat,
> Wont hang their craigs, we also O Adamu might
> Shelter the while our sun-scourged stricken pates.
> O for those broad cool sappy leaves of EDEN!
>
> (54)

The ugliness of "craigs" and "pates" clashes disagreeably with the
smoother and more tactile "broad cool sappy leaves" as Doughty's style
reinforces the contrast inherent in the content.

When Adam and Adama finally attain the Field promised by God
and find shelter in a cave, the pleasure they experience in these simple
comforts is actually greater than that offered by Eden because it is
heightened by a knowledge of bad things lacking in Eden. Sleep is
good because it has been earned; safety joyful because dangers have
been overcome to achieve it:

> The LORD is good, to-night the LORD
> Hath shut us in, in safety, with our fold. . . .
> . . . Thou HAWWA hast
> Need thou to sleep: sleep! whiles I bete our hearth.
>
> (123–24)

Doughty's simple and sensual language throughout the poem, combined with his fresh insights into ordinary experience, manage to rec-
oncile us to the Fall and to the earth we live on by treating our life
as—in the senior James's words—a "rise to the normal human level."
In the form of a journey allegory, he has succeeded in capturing a great
alteration of consciousness from superhuman to human, and allows us
to see normal human life with new eyes.

IX   *Doughty and Adam*

Doughty has managed to give us in this poem the inner change in
him caused by his travels in Arabia and which is not clearly indicated
in *Arabia Deserta*. We feel "This dizzy withering heat" and see the
"Thick wárm salt living blood" (*Adam*, 74) that actually fell from

Doughty's own nostrils when he was pressed in a hard physical test in Arabia, as we read in *Arabia Deserta*. But even more, we feel the contraction and purification of consciousness caused by his travels. As Murry has brilliantly commented:

Adam Cast Forth is in essence a sublime simplification of all that he [Doughty] lived and learned in the Arabian desert. There he had become as the first man; under that implacable sun he had been as it were dissolved away into an elemental essence of mortality, he had become the I AM of man, the plaything yet the equal of his own ineffable but jealous God.[22]

Put simply, in Arabia Doughty was reduced to the lowest possible denominator of his being: the land was stripped bare of all comforting green and water; he was pressed physically to the end by hardship and bilharzia; he had to defend his life almost every day; he was cut off from all support from his own culture; and he had to be alone with himself as never before, even for an orphan a hard task.

He must have wondered what kind of God it was that had put into his mind the irresistible urge to undertake this hard journey, what kind of God it was who, supposedly loving according to Christianity, had created a world as harsh as that he had to face. But like a mystic he learned not rebellion and dissent, but acceptance and spiritual purification through hard trials: his inner core was equal to the task of standing alone for these years, and he came through the journey alive. Like the "old hermits of Christian faith ... devising in themselves to retrieve the first Adam in their own souls" about whom we read in *Arabia Deserta* (I, 473), Doughty clarified and strengthened his Christian beliefs, his sense of his own abilities and weaknesses, and his view of the essential and unessential during this journey. There was a benevolent God whose tests and chastisement of man led to greater strength.

So with Adam. He becomes fit to father mankind only after he has been thoroughly tested by the conditions of this world, rather than Eden's ease. Ishmael of Melville's *Moby Dick*, another lonely Adamic man self-forced into the ocean in order to discover the proper way to live, learned that felicity lies "in the wife, the heart, the bed, the table, the saddle, the fireside, the country," rather than in more extreme experiences. Similarly, Doughty's Adam and Adama find strength and redemption in their relationship; and Doughty himself had married after his Arabian travels, in 1886, becoming an exemplary husband and father.

X   *Anglo-Arabian versus American Adam*

Critics have pointed out the basic similarity between Doughty's
Adam and Milton's: the title of Doughty's poem (adopted when the
publisher rejected his original title, *Hawwa*) signifies a continuation of
Milton's *Paradise Lost*, and the scene in which Adama views herself
in the pool for the first time comes into Doughty's poem from Milton's.
Yet the same critics—particularly Anne Treneer and Middleton
Murry—have been quick to state that the two poems present few like-
nesses of form or content beyond the basic parallels. When we think
of *Adam Cast Forth*'s lines—"Those be the generations of thy Sons;
/ That shall be in multitude, as the leaves of grass. / But what now
seest thou Adam, in thy Vision?" (86)—another poetic parallel, closer
to Doughty's own period, inescapably comes to mind. Although it is
highly doubtful that Doughty read Walt Whitman's *Leaves of Grass*,
the surprising similarities in outlook between the two Adamic poets
remind us once again that Doughty has a certain affinity with other
Victorian poets, and help us define Doughty's uniqueness more closely.

Although Doughty is more puritanical about sex, respectful of tradition, and more austere than Whitman, he shares in this poem Whitman's attempt to make us see with the eyes of Adam, to penetrate to
a new, "primitive" view of the world. He does not sound a "barbaric
yawp" but he does enable us to understand what it might have been
like to be Adam, which is Whitman's goal as well. Where Whitman
broke the poetic line and did away with meter, Doughty typically
came up with the opposite approach, utilizing the oldest words he
could find to recreate the oldest experience of mankind and becoming
new in his radical antiquarianism. Doughty loved tradition too much
ever to conceive of free verse, but the radical oldness of his style of
Hebrew words (and his use of biblical parallelisms for a "primitive"
effect, also employed by Whitman) is intended to accomplish the same
result of breaking through the consciousness of the present into the
past. Like Whitman, Doughty is in this poem a "chanter of Adamic
songs" *(Children of Adam)* of love between man and woman, who
seeks to go "back, back to wisdom's birth, to innocent intuitions, /
Again with fair creation" *(Passage to India)*. Doughty's simple style
captures the same pretraditional feeling as Whitman's free verse, if in
a more quiet manner.

We can see Doughty in this poem as a puritanical, English Whitman
whose goal was to recreate and rival the Bible's living experience in

new works rather than to write his own, completely new Bible as Whitman did. In maintaining the basic image of a traditional God whose decrees may not be questioned, a puritanical prudishness which does not mention sexual matters openly, and a more or less traditional blank verse, Doughty's narrowly original "sacred drama" has a certain stodginess implicit in the subtitle, which reminds us of many boringly pious products of the last century. Even in his most original, Eastern, and authentically "old" poem, we glimpse some Revival aspects that will not stand qualitative comparison with Whitman's new skyscraper.

If we wished, we could also criticize *Adam Cast Forth*'s thin literal side of the allegory, the Bunyanesque Valleys of Vision and Rest that never come alive outside of their names; the Satan who makes little trouble after a promising opening; the inconsistent God who asks Adam to request what he will and then refuses to cancel "lives' taint" when Adam asks him to do so, and who is generally a bore, as Gods will be; and all the choruses consisting of nothing but bald praise of an abstract God-voice who never comes alive.

But somehow, Doughty makes us forget these questions and faults as we read the poem. Although below Whitman's total originality and Milton's power and complexity of thought, *Adam Cast Forth* represents the high point of Doughty's poetry. He achieves an almost Blakean compression and simplicity and manages to make us *feel* his own experience of living as Adam Cast Forth: "he is such who has a clean human heart and long-suffering under his bare shirt" (*Arabia Deserta*, I, 56). It is also a unique poem. Doughty's Adam, seen as the first actual human being, is as original in his way as Khalil is in his. As he and Hawwa move before us with the slow, concentrated effect of a medieval tableau, we have more of a feeling that we know how Adam might actually have been than we gain from any other English poem. In *Adam Cast Forth*, Doughty pushes his quest for the past and for past language to its deepest human reach, attaining to depths of his own consciousness and ours not touched elsewhere in his poetic corpus.

XI   Mansoul: *Introduction and Plot*

When *Mansoul Or The Riddle of the World* appeared in 1920, Doughty was almost eighty years old. He revised it in order to produce a second edition in 1923—making his style more concrete, his treatment of the Crucifixion oblique but rapturous, as in *Dawn in Britain*, and his expression in the Arabia episode more bald, as Fairley points out—and was working on more revisions at the time of his death, as his much annotated 1923 *Mansoul* in the Gonville and Caius Library shows. Doughty felt that he had not solved "The Riddle of the World" which constitutes the poem's theme, and many of his readers agree: Fairley and John Holloway see *Mansoul* as the inferior product of old age in a declining line from the high point of *Dawn in Britain*. But Doughty himself thought it his best poem and the writer of the *London Times* obituary (22 January 1926) calls it a "comprehensive morality, perhaps his poetic masterpiece."

If *Mansoul*'s thought is clichéd and platitudinous and lacks the narrative clothing that exists in *Dawn* and *Adam*, its style and tone are far more relaxed and mellow than those of its predecessors and Doughty seems more at peace with himself and the world, despite a brief fulmination against the kaiser for World War I. Its title, which sounds much like an Arabic word, *mansour*, meaning "rendered victorious by God," which is in turn related to the root from which *Nasrâny*, or Christian, derives, becomes a complex multilingual pun. In English, "Mansoul" refers to the town of Mansoul ("Man's Soul") in Bunyan's *Holy War*. Thus, the English meaning and the Arabic sound of the word together connote a specifically Christian victory over sin in the struggle for man's soul. Despite his conscious attempt at religious universality in this poem, Doughty's title indicates its true Christian message which is in fact what we find in the poem itself. As poet-speaker, Doughty gives us directly his conclusions about life's questions for us to accept or reject.

In book 1, "The Muses Garden," the poet falls into a musing trance—reminiscent of the medieval dream-journey of *Piers Plowman* for instance—and finds himself transported to another world. He asks the fundamental question of the whole poem, "What were indeed right paths of a mans feet, / That lacking light, wont stumble in Worlds murk?"[23] and journeys to the underworld in company with Minimus, an Everyman-like hermit into whose personality he sometimes blends, and with Mansoul, the Byronic quester, in search of an answer. We follow the trio through a series of shifting scenes which constitute the rest of the poem, and the dream framework only partially excuses their lack of order and smooth transitions.

In book 2, "The Descent," Doughty and Minimus accompany Mansoul through an unoriginal house of the dead which comprises a colorless limbo of labyrinthine tunnels lacking the complexity—and interest—of Dante's cosmic structure, for instance. Along with dead sinners, whose major fault is "Self-love" (39), Doughty meets the dead British soldiers of World War I and embarks on one of the "patriotic" paeans that mar all his poetic work except *Adam Cast Forth*. However, he recovers enough of the universal spirit which he tries to make dominant in this poem to quote the goddess Hertha who says that "The pathways óf the Just, in áll the Earth; / Shall meet together in One Holy Place" (45–46). But we cannot help noticing that Britain's soldiers are automatically just, while no German soldiers ever appear to be.

The three travelers meet Zarathustra, who advises them to "Walk in the ways of Truth, eschew dark paths" (58), a good if overly abstract and therefore meaningless admonition, as are most of the others that appear in *Mansoul*. What is Truth? What are "dark paths"? Since no concrete case is ever given, Doughty's famous sages offer us only the same broad doubletalk that we get from a fortune-teller who will not commit himself to a particular, precise prophecy. And by making philosophers of all creeds utter the same vague message, Doughty reveals his inability or lack of desire to consider non-Christian religious messages and can remain fixed in his devotion to Christianity from the start without ever entering into controversy.

Thus, in book 3, "The Radious Rocks," Buddha and Confucius give the trio the same abstract moralism as Zarathustra: "Eschew all crooked paths . . ." (72). Through the voices of the Fates, Doughty admits a measure of cultural relativity, allowing that Reason is "warped, with every variance of the World" (78) and is not uniform in every place and time, but what this means is that he is willing to accept other pathways to truth, as long as they accord with his Christian and scientific beliefs.

As in *Arabia Deserta*, but with less justification since *Mansoul* is a work of fiction, places follow on one another without a causal principle. Suddenly we find ourselves in Arabia ("A weary ground, which seldom shadowed is, / . . . which stiffened lies as bronze," 79), then Petra ("Behold a Valley of Tombs, hewn in sand-rock," 85), and finally in a harsh Sinai desert ("What horror of bergs aloft! /. . . Gladly it we forsake, and further pass," 86), as the East brings out once again some of Doughty's best writing. The book concludes with an Egypt under "Right and Just" (88) British rule and an Egyptian priest's admonition to give alms.

Book 4, "Great Underworld's Voyage," which includes an interview with a Socrates who notes that no one knows "whether Gods made men, or Man made Gods" (103), is notable for the implicit clash between Doughty's religious beliefs and his science and the fact that he makes no attempt to resolve it. His view of the Old Testament is very "scientific" and rational: the history of Israel amounts to tribal warfare ("As they allege, commanded of their God," 105) and David appears as merely "A climbing spirit and founden stout in fight" (106), which accords with the view expressed by Doughty's King James annotations, as we have seen.

Jesus however is described thus:

> Words that He taught, were words of deathless Life:
> Such being as no mans lips, before His, spake.
> Words which sown in mens hearts, left ever sith;
> Souls from Earths dust, to Heavenly Fatherhood.
>
> (107)

Although Doughty in this poem speaks of universal values, Jesus receives clear preference to Buddha, Confucius, Socrates, and all the other wise men. Moses and Mohammed are conspicuous by their absence; so is Solomon. Jesus receives more space than anyone else and at the end of the poem only his words are inscribed over the gateway to the next world.

We see that Doughty views Jesus with the passion of a true believer. His character Mansoul addresses the "ALL-FATHER" (120) reverently, as we would expect. But then Mansoul suddenly stands proudly on science as an impossible-to-contradict religion: "There come is látely untó mens hands, / a BOOK; / A Book of Truth, which none can contradict; / Sith Heavens High Finger it háth bóth wrought and writ" (121). We see the nineteenth-century geologist existing side by side with the pious believer in Doughty's mind, and he makes no attempt to bring the two things together clearly. A scientist can be religious certainly, but it would have been interesting to know exactly where Doughty stood on the question of Darwin for instance, where science and religion were pulling against one another. From *Arabia Deserta*, we can infer a vague idea, as Richard Bevis does, that Doughty made a very personal use of Darwin and geology to prove God's existence. But in what purports to be a meditative poem, Doughty has an obligation to consider the science versus religion question more deeply and openly than his generalities allow, and to demonstrate rather than assert his conclusions.

We are in any case forced abruptly to leave Mansoul's unresolved statements as Doughty brings up World War I, which he blames on "Hunnish enemies" (126) who follow a "mountebank criminal" (129), the kaiser, who evilly opposes England's "magnanimous sons" and "Britains sovereign, (GODS true knight, / Belovéd óf his People)" (131). In Doughty's belief that Britain had "with GOD, the World to save" (132), he returns to his old simpleminded intolerance and almost ruins completely the fragile universality that he has painfully labored to establish in the poem. Perhaps fortunately the book ends here and book 5, "From Underworld Returned. A Day of the Sun," is a far more happy and less contradictory affair.

This book finds Doughty awakening from his dream of death, destruction, and national glory to console himself with his English Muse once again. He becomes Minimus, least of men, and sees Caedmon, the Old English poet, tell a tale of Bloodaxe and his battles that, unfortunately, lacks substance. He has a vision of Titans, then elves, fairies, and dwarfs and their ruler King Oberon. Doughty upon Oberon's death takes farewell of the elves who appear in his poetry and who symbolize a former golden age of England and, we feel, of Doughty's own youth.

As a consolation for the loss of Oberon, he now sees Mansoul's dream city of human hope. Mansoul, now returned from death, announces the failure of his quest for ultimate answers, but some voices express hope that "In time to come . . . more light shall shine" (202). Book 5 ends on this note of hopeful resignation:

> The Sum of all is, There be many paths;
> Of Mans endeavour, seeking RIGHTEOUSNESS;
> Wherein, reborn, a soul may fearless walk;
> Towards the Infinite Unknown, in eternal paths.
>   (203)

The final book 6 reveals "Mansouls Dream City" in greater detail. Doughty-Minimus hears Greek philosophers state the value of renunciation, "But little had they wrought of wórthy work" (209). He then comes upon astronomers who try to chronicle "The supreme works" (210) of God, but these "Can only, in empty ciphers" (211) express the meaning of the universe. So science is no answer after all. After a young man describes an eruption of Etna like the Vesuvian explosion which Doughty himself witnessed, a group of scientists agree that "Like as a seed, / All that is, works, though hid, and moves and tends

/ Circling, without cease, meeting, without end" (218). The poet-speaker praises engineers who apply the power of the gods to benefit men.

Doughty now hears two young men discuss poetry. They praise Chaucer, except for his sexually explicit passages, and say that a poet's task is to "modulate; / What measures noblest are in human heart" (224). There follows the long comparison of poetry and Gothic cathedrals that calls Victorian Gothic to mind in connection with *Mansoul* and Doughty's other poems. He leaves this conversation and finally finds himself in a temple of all nations presided over by an aged priest. As souls enter the death state through a door, he reads on its lintel:

> FEAR YE NOT LITTLE FLOCK: and underneath,
> HATH NOT JESHÛA SAID THAT GOD IS LOVE.
> (Words, which abide, a PERFUME, in our hearts.)
>   (240)

XII   Mansoul *as Meditative Epic*

In *Mansoul*, Doughty resorted to the Victorian genre of the meditative epic. Herman Melville, Richard Burton, and William Gifford Palgrave, fellow Eastern travelers, also set down their life-philosophies in long poems which appear to us to be an irritating addiction of their period, far less exciting than romantic laudanum dreams. But Melville's *Clarel* (1876), Burton's *Kasidah of Haji Abdu El-Yezdi* (1880), and Palgrave's *Vision of Life* (1891) do highlight Doughty's lack of sophistication as a thinker.

Melville embarks on an Arnoldian dialogue between faith and doubt as he subjects Christianity to a piercing scrutiny through the points of view of his character Clarel and his fellow pilgrims in a desolate Holy Land. His capacity for wide-ranging speculation enables him to sum up the perplexities of the post-Darwinian period:

> Yea, ape and angel, strife and old debate—
> The harps of heaven and the dreary gongs of hell;
> Science the feud can only aggravate—
> No umpire she betwixt the chimes and knell:
> The running battle of the star and clod
> Shall run forever—if there be no God.

Although his poem has its many dull moments, no one can claim that Melville has not done his best to face his time courageously and deeply in an effort to find a way to live.

Burton's *Kasidah*, though purposely conventional in its eight-syllable lines and couplets and use of contractions and abstractions in order to imitate vaguely an Arabic style, reveals its author's brilliant knowledge of languages and comparative religions, sharp wit, and independent thought. Burton explains and dismisses Sufi mysticism, Christianity, Buddhism, Jainism, and Hinduism among other philosophies before deciding in favor of "Self-cultivation, with due regard to others," as a final life-philosophy. His poem attains the charm of Fitzgerald's *Rubaiyat of Omar Khayyam* while far surpassing in depth Fitzgerald-Omar's superficial materialism and hedonism.

Gifford Palgrave's *A Vision of Life* totally denies his age's belief in Progress by asserting a decline of civilization since a Golden Age in the far past; in the first book of his poem he even asserts that Christianity, having appeared when the world was already deteriorating, is a degenerate religion. Although the last two books become Christian and then openly Catholic in accordance with the author's reconversion to this faith, we see a mind capable of ranging widely over complex matters.

All three poems suffer from too many capitalized abstractions and rather boring jingly rhyme-schemes; all three (except perhaps *Clarel*) are as unread today as *Mansoul*. But no reader can fail to be impressed by the range of intellect displayed by each writer. *Mansoul*, by contrast, lacks sophistication, depth, and subtlety. It disappoints by raising expectations of answers to major issues and then failing to provide them outside of a few platitudes which are constantly repeated. Doughty fails to face up to the science-religion controversy tackled head-on by Melville; and he lacked the ability of all three to question deeply the faith in which he was born. His knowledge of other religious traditions is superficial to say the least, each of the sages in the poem stating the same simpleminded advice to "eschew crooked paths." The East has left a greater impact on the intellects of Doughty's colleagues, but—if *Adam Cast Forth* be considered—Doughty was far more emotionally affected than they. In a meditative poem, however, intellect is the more important quality.

It becomes clear after reading his traveling contemporaries that Doughty, however diligently he wanted to know the universe's answers, was not intellectually equipped to find them. Part of *Arabia*

Deserta's greatness is that it suggests and implies but never like the
poetry disappoints through metaphysical simplemindedness; the narrator's voice in the prose work is more intelligent, if prejudiced, and is
always qualified by the actions and characters in any case. But if
Doughty as a poet discovers only conventional wisdom, there are worse
philosophies, and the impulse toward a questing mind is there. If he
never reconciles science and religion we understand that this inability—or lack of desire—is a characteristic of his mind. If he does not
quite achieve a truly universal point of view, *Mansoul* still reflects his
most energetic, conscious attempt to develop one. And his shock that
World War I could occur in his "enlightened" times ("A flood poured
out, of murdered human gore: / And in these days of ours," 127) is
more of a sad comment on the times than on his continuously optimis-
tic approach to life.

XIII   Mansoul: *Style*

Doughty's failure to be an interesting thinker is almost forgivable in
this poem, perhaps because with *Adam Cast Forth* it is his most
relaxed and readable. By writing more straightforward lines than
Dawn in Britain's and by easing the unusual words and constructions,
he comes closer to the reader and farther from his early poetic theories
that demanded in *Dawn in Britain* a high-pitched, sometimes hopelessly awkward tone no matter how trivial the action or how lacking in
poetic insight a given passage. Yet *Mansoul* maintains Doughty's stylistic individuality. The word "Perfume," used to describe Jesus's
words, most perfectly describes the style of this poem. The first book
is full of delicate filigree work, like "Broods o'er those thymy eyots
drowsy hum; / Bourdon of glistening bees, in mails of gold" (12). The
fifth book contains this delicate description of the fairy queen's palace:

> In wonder of íts fóur white radious walls;
> Glittering with pearly stars: the carven squames,
> One over other laid, of oyster-shales.
>
> (191)

Barker Fairley and John Holloway have seen in Doughty's heavy
use of accent marks in *Mansoul* proof of his poetic decline. Yet the
visual aspect of these accents lends a real charm to the poem, and since
they make no difference to the reader who does not speak the lines,

they are rather a positive aspect and are certainly unique, of a piece with Doughty's refusal to use apostrophes for the possessive. Furthermore, he uses such accents in all his poems, if not so heavily. We have, as Holloway claims, passages of conventional poetic diction in *Mansoul*, but conventional passages are very frequently present in *Dawn in Britain* as well: "Moreo'er king Brennus" (146); "Lifted, on immense wings, flew Rumour forth" (541); "Yet monstrous demon saw I, shake those cliffs, / Strong Spirit of Storm" (192). As we have seen, Walter Bezanson's comment on *Clarel's* conventional language applies to Doughty's poetry as well. As Holloway himself admits, he is comparing Doughty's "early work at its best and his later verse at its worst,"[24] thus doing less than justice to *Mansoul*. The fact is that Doughty's major poems have some strong and more weak passages and are thus typical of the long poems written in his age.

At his best, Doughty in *Mansoul* writes passages just as memorable as the strong passages of *Dawn*, but manages a greater fluency and ease:

> Lay Spring-times golden smile, all gracious mild,
> On dunes and denes there likewise, óf Gods ground.
> After long Winters teen, sweet is this breath,
> Of blossomed boughs and mantle of tender green,
> In field and heath; whereón now softly blows,
> Whitening each spire of grass, attempered wind.
> And heavens loft rings, with ditty of lavrocks voice.
>
> (164)

In addition to such nature passages, we have the lines about Arabia and Sinai, the cathedral metaphor, and the fairy episodes. Of course, these are not enough to save the poem, just as *Dawn's* good passages do not save it. Although *Mansoul's* desultory structure is not so irritating because it has the excuse of mirroring a dream, we cannot praise Doughty for improved structural ability; and his characters and their message are too abstract and clichéd to be truly meaningful. Compared to *Adam Cast Forth*, there is too much "thought" and not enough sensing in this poem. And while *Dawn in Britain's* style is too twisted and high-pitched for its frequently lightweight action and melodramatic heroics, *Mansoul's* thought is too emptily clichéd to permit more than very infrequent poetic insights of a memorable kind.

We come back to the cathedral metaphor with which Doughty ends

Mansoul. Especially in the realm of thought, but also to some degree in genteel-antiquarian language as well, Doughty's poems—with the exception of the truly autobiographical and powerful *Adam Cast Forth*—are too much, rather than too little, of their age. Doughty failed to recreate the perfect Gothic cathedral and instead produced a weird but frequently dull and awkward imitation, like many of his architectural contemporaries. The value of his major poetry, however, resides in the exploratory attempt to recapture the past and the lessons of his successes and failures for future poets.

CHAPTER 6

New Worlds:
The Cliffs, The Clouds, The Titans

IN *The Cliffs* (1909), *The Clouds* (1912), and *The Titans* (1916),
Doughty totally sacrificed even the attempt at linguistic complexity
and complexity of vision characteristic of high art in order to concentrate on straightforward plot. The first two works, written to warn
England of impending war with Germany, combine all the melodramatic and structural weaknesses of the major poems with a fanatic
chauvinism—including child sacrifice in *The Cliffs*—surpassing even
that of *Under Arms* and the attack on the kaiser in *Mansoul*. When
Doughty tries to view his own times with the Caradoc-like attitudes of
the past, he reveals himself as more of a British tribal barbarian than
any of his "fanatic" Moslems ever was, and more cruelly patriotic than
the King David whose actions he had scored with disapproving exclamation marks in his Bible.

But Doughty was an apostle of technological if not what we would
now consider social progress. In its blurbs for the poems, Duckworth's
(Doughty's publisher) touted them as "POEMS THAT FORETOLD THE
WAR."[1] Doughty's prophecy of World War I in both poems, and his
vision of what we now know as sonar, lasers, submarines, airplanes, and
new explosives, mark him as a serious science-fiction precursor. True,
he was not alone in this. In 1907, H. G. Wells in his *The War in the
Air* predicted that Germany would attack America only for both to be
overwhelmed by a Japanese and Chinese alliance. If Doughty ever
went to the cinema, he might have seen the British film *The Airship
Destroyer* (1909) by Charles Urban, which features a London attacked
by dirigibles and the use of radio controlled aerial torpedoes, or its
imitator, *The Aerial Anarchists* (1911), which again showed airships
bombing London. Doughty is just as technologically imaginative as
(and far more politically accurate than) the writers of these works, but
The Cliffs and *The Clouds* have not received the credit for science-

fiction invention that they deserve. It is also interesting to watch how Doughty's use of conventional fairies and elves goes hand in hand with his modern fantasy of technology in these two poems. Rarely has the connection between science fiction and earlier forms of fantasy been so clearly, if awkwardly, demonstrated.

The *Titans* is a geological allegory of man's technological conquest of the earth's energy sources. Seen in terms of high art, it is a too-abstract descriptive poem that never comes alive, lacking as it does even a single human hero. However, the visualization of the battle between Titans and gods and the evolution of life on earth is amazingly similar to the presentation of dinosauric battles in Walt Disney's *Fantasia* or King Kong's or Godzilla's depredations, for that matter. Except for the stagey poetic language we could be watching a science-fiction horror film.

Although they lack totally the force of the good moments in the major poetry and remain on the level of comic books, Doughty's "earth" (rather than "space") operas should be recovered as important early examples of science fiction, in which we see him as anxiously questing for the future as he had earlier for the past, or (in *The Titans*) showing how the past leads to the future. We see the concern for England's coming days that had earlier led Doughty to search out the ruins in Arabia.

I   The Cliffs

In this "Drama of the Time, in Five Parts," three German soldiers—called "Persanians"—land on the English coast in a balloon as a scouting party. They discuss Britain's cultural, political, and military weaknesses and the Persanian preparations for a full-scale invasion to begin the next day by air and sea. When the stereotypically wicked baron who leads the group is confronted by John Hobbe, a retired British soldier turned shepherd, he stabs Hobbe, saying "Die peasant swine."[2] This comic-book line is only slightly less improbable than Hobbe's delivering of a patriotic oration to the tune of thunder and lightning as he raises himself on one elbow before dying. But the airship and the submarine have been futuristically mentioned.

In part 2, the action moves to a more "allegorical" level as we see "Brittanias Temple" through a mist, with the words "Religion" and "Patriotism" inscribed on it in fading letters. "Britain's Truth," following the orders of Sirion, a godlike creature, instructs his elves to begin weighing souls in preparation for arousing Britain. Truth tells us that priests' souls, which could help Britain, have been oppressed by "The cockney malice of mad Parliaments" which tax them "out of life" (88), and the elves report that the souls of the Imperial Military Council are worthless.

We return to literal action in part 3 as the coast guard finds Hobbe's body along with the Persanian invasion plans and other improbable clues. A fisherman reports that the Persanian balloon was struck by lightning (the same that God caused while Hobbe was speaking no doubt) and all three Persanians in it are dead; the baron has been killed by falling on the same sword he had used to murder Hobbe. The fisherman's verdict sums up Doughty's idea of divine justice as expressed in this play: "If were, as some think, spies them foreign soldiers; / Hath visited them the heavy Hand of God!" (126–27). British airmen report having seen the Persanian fleet preparing to sail, there are attempts to telegraph the bumbling Admiralty (which is closed on Sunday of course), and Hobbe's aged widow, children, and dog go crying past his body. The Persanians block Portsmouth and Medway harbors, but London is finally alerted and the Empire begins to despatch troops. Doughty's invention of "othismometers," or sonar, which reads the pulse of enemy propellers, redeems this act to some extent.

Part 4 shows the "Sacred Band," Doughty's childish secret service, swearing to "Kiss death! and covet all to die for Britain" (214), on the orders of their Hierophant or high priest. He says that only the sacrifice of an infant by its widowed mother will lift the blinds from Britain's eyes, and Widow Charity eagerly steps forward to offer hers, claiming "Himself, with smiles, he gives" (241)! The child dies as "Sanctá Britannia" is sung by "women-souls' voices" and "Brittanias Image increaseth in majesty and brightness" (244) as a result of this human sacrifice. The elves decide to embalm the child in honey. Just as the Sacred Band, through such useful actions as this sacrifice, prepares to save Britain, the ruler of Persania recalls his fleet, apparently having found Britain too staunchly defended.

As the Persanian navy puts back in part 5, its two largest battleships hit their own mines and sink with heavy loss of life, and Hobbe's fellow villagers join in a hearty patriotic singsong during which the vicar embraces the flag as he sings. The highlights of this act are a new explosive called Kratite, mines made of glass, a weapon called a Katera that can bring down a regiment at a mile's distance, chemical shells, airplanes, and perhaps most amazingly a laserlike neutron beam which sends light through the armor of ships and numbs their crews.

For a man of peace and father of two daughters, Doughty had

become remarkably adept at planning battles (beginning with *Dawn in Britain*) and forecasting new weapons of war. In contrast to the peaceable masochism of Khalil in *Arabia Deserta*, we have in *The Cliffs* an open, fanatic sadism. As Middleton Murry wrote of Widow Charity's child sacrifice, "Doughty had come to be unconscious of the distinction between patriotism and Moloch worship. . . . The man who could make fairies condone that inhuman sacrifice had become estranged from the country he loved: his zeal had eaten him up."[3] And T. E. Lawrence in a letter to Mrs. Charlotte Shaw privately reveals his view of *The Cliffs, The Titans*, and the anti-German portions of *Mansoul* in no uncertain terms: "They give me the creeps. Such fanatic love and hatred ought not to be. Who are we to judge? I don't believe even God can."[4] Under the influence of a possible war, Doughty had forgotten what he himself had written in *Arabia Deserta* years earlier: "Patriotism and Religion! In the one and the other there seem to us to be sweetly comprehended all virtues; and yet in the excess they are springs from which flow out extreme mischiefs!" (I, 549). Even *Arabia Deserta*'s very patriotic narrator never imagined excesses like those approved by Doughty in *The Cliffs*.

Doughty's writing in *The Cliffs* is almost as grotesque as his "thought." The "evil" baron is not described, but we have seen his arrogant monocle glinting in the pages of a thousand comic books. He and the "good" Persanians of the scouting party, Lieutenant Weise and Hans—who argue in favor of Britain, even approving its Boer War concentration camps (41)—reveal Doughty's inability to visualize the enemy as other than anti- or philo-, in short his inability to see them as human beings. In all fairness, his British characters are not much more believable: Hobbe is as loyal as his old dog and as stupid for revealing himself to the Persanian scouts. The heroic British aeronauts and Captain Pakenham are hopelessly "straight"; we can see their rosy cheeks and shining eyes in the same comic books in which evil German barons appear. Widow Charity is no less than a monster, as are the elves who rejoice in her deed. The dialogue spoken by the characters is contemporary but stagily stilted and full of awkward "poetic" inversions: "when . . . / . . . you've some spare weekend, or more: / you'll honour us, it spending at my house" (252). It is as improbable for expressing modern action as the action of the play itself: the Persanians who are so efficiently warlike leave behind all their plans and clues when their balloon takes off, and the much-maligned Admiralty efficiently gets soldiers to the coast within a few hours. Elves, fairies, prophetic dreams, and Brittanias Temple do not fit with Kratite and laser beams, although the combination does awkwardly and unconsciously reveal the connection between older pastoral and science fantasy.

If contemporary British literature—which included Hardy, James, and Yeats, and soon was to include Joyce and D. H. Lawrence, all of whom Doughty never read—was for Doughty "Brain-wasting rant, and narrow melting plaint!" (46) and "The vice of hunch-back Spirits and blighted hearts" (46), *The Cliffs* is not calculated to remedy the situation. But if we consciously put aside literary and philosophical judgments, and read the play for its technological imagination only, we will find it the intriguing equivalent of a 1909 comic book.

II The Clouds

As German-British rivalry increased, Doughty grew more and more convinced that he must play the role of *vates,* or poet-seer, and warn his nation. *The Cliffs,* quite predictably, had failed to arouse Britain, and so *The Clouds,* a more concrete but still flawed vision, appeared in 1912. In this poetic drama, Britain's Muse grants a Doughty who sometimes blends into a young poet, Colin (named for Doughty's hero, Spenser), a glimpse at possible future history. Doughty-Colin witnesses the journey of one Edward Carpenter through an England invaded and partially occupied by "Eastlanders," or Germans. Carpenter experiences all the trials of life in an invaded and defeated country— destruction, social dislocation, anarchy, dictatorship, economic depression, and even a new disease, "war-dread,"[5] which causes "*kardiorhexis,*" or heart attacks. Carpenter's own home is occupied by drunken Eastlander soldiers and he dies of exhaustion before he finds his mother, the goal of his search.

The only counterbalance to this picture of gloom lies in the exploits of the Sacred Band (carried over from *The Cliffs*), who hold out some suggestion of guerrilla warfare against the triumphant enemy. Sister Gertrude, a priestess of patriotic British sentiment, urges the weary fighters on with a hearty "Doubt not to die the death of Patriots!" (70), and serves as one of the "woman riders" who take part, vaguely, in battles themselves.

As in *The Cliffs,* Doughty's technological prescience remains impressive even when his writing is not: he predicts a death-ray of "wireless venimous waves" (52) made in the United States, able to destroy a whole country, "irradiating counter waves" able to "jam" telegraph messages (91), and high speed "torpedo boats." And his visualization of the enemy's precise plan of invasion is very plausible.

Although *The Clouds* is far from a good poem, it represents an advance over *The Cliffs* in concrete vision and the subordination of overt rhetoric to dramatic action. Since no enemy except a drunken major ever speaks, Doughty has no opportunity to portray Eastlanders in *The Cliff*'s evil-monocle terms. Although there is no reason for Carpenter to die exactly where he does, or for his revelation of his background toward the end of the poem rather than at its beginning, or for most other events to happen precisely when they do, we are somewhat inclined to accept this structural haphazardness in what is a dream-collage of war scenes. Elf scenes and an Izaak Walton pastoral passage appear extraneous and jarring because they are too far removed from the level of literal action—as in the case of the "allegorical" sections of *The Cliffs*—but we understand that Doughty wanted to contrast peaceful British life with the horrors of war. The level of ideas is not much higher than that of *The Cliffs*, with the Sacred Band's death-vow still in force and the vicar in the camp of fugitives who advises soldiers to enjoy getting wounded and dying for their country. Doughty's rejection of Communism is no surprise, and on pages 46–47 we see the only overt mention of this doctrine in all his works. But we have no child sacrifices and his attack on Parliament is less savagely stated than in *The Cliffs*.

The emphasis remains on the simple horror of Britain invaded, and Doughty succeeds to some degree in making his visualization of social breakdown and new, horrible weapons real. Like a good science-fiction writer, he gives us a convincing "what if" picture, even if his prophecy of invasion never came true. The complexity of historical forces that lead to wars was beyond Doughty's power to grasp here, as in *The Cliffs* and *The Dawn in Britain*. As Samuel Chew has commented on *The Cliffs* and *The Clouds*, "Intense moral indignation and austere patriotism are combined with a naive belief in the absolute justice of his country's cause and the utter malignities of her enemies."[6] But if the "why" escapes Doughty, he manages to present the "how" in *The Clouds*. Despite the falsely "poetic" language, sentimentality of false heroics, poorly realized characters (including Carpenter), lack of deep thought—what are the *causes* of the war? in no place do we learn—and meandering structure, the poem comes off a shade better than *The Cliffs*.

Early reviewers compared this poem to Hardy's *Dynasts*, although

Doughty indignantly denied knowing even Hardy's name. The difference between the two dramatic poems is perhaps more obvious than the "epic" similarity noted by the reviewers: even Hardy's crude philosophic objectivity which treats all events and nations with a uniform irony rather than with heroic grandeur was beyond Doughty's grasp, and saves Hardy from Doughty's naive chauvinism. For its prediction of World War I, *The Clouds* will maintain its position as one of the curiosities of literature, but it will never be more than that.

III   The Titans

The *Titans* tells the story of man's technological conquest of nature's forces. In the center of the earth, the Titans are spontaneously created. Demons enter them, giving them life and vaguely human shapes. At the same moment, heaven implants the seeds of plant and animal life on earth in the form of a "jelly-dew."[7] The Titans fall into a lifeless state, and man is created (through a vague, undefined process), and develops speech, weapons, and laws. When the Titans awaken, they challenge men for mastery of the earth. In a "titanic" battle they are defeated by the gods, men's allies, before they can arrive at Mantown, and are put to sleep.

Following a heavenly forecast of earthquakes, men move from Mantown, crossing deserts, before they come to Eden, a fruitful field prepared for them by the gods. A golden age ensues, during which a shepherd discovers writing and teaches it to the priests. But bad times of pestilence and war come too. Finally, God orders a return to tranquillity and speech is perfected, allowing high-level thought. One day, hunters from Eden accidentally find the old Mantown and the still slumbering Titans and their allies the giants. Like the Lilliputians going after Gulliver, young men from one of Eden's towns succeed in bringing a giant back. He is buried to his loins, tied down, and made to work for the town, while "Children of men him mock and brave around!" (152). The giant's one eye is blind, and despite Doughty's admonition that "Man lightens thus his burden of this Worlds smart" (153), the picture of the mocked giant is sad, recalling Samson's plight. Other towns get the idea and each brings back its own giant to exploit. The temple-city, Gate-of-God, raises a Titan, not merely a giant, and thus gains dominion over all the other cities when it harnesses his power.

We are told that man will one day classify and measure all—lands, animals, and birds—just as Doughty did in Arabia. But his scientific pride is qualified by a last religious thought that man is "yet unweaned, untaught, unworth" (161). Perhaps the most interesting thing in the whole book is Doughty's vision of atomic work (which reveals that he had been reading about Einstein, which is possible by 1916): "The adamantine Elements; / Couched indivisible particles; ... / ... At his list; / He unbinds them, and anew upknits" (159–60).

The *Titans* most fully summarizes Doughty's life-interests. It explores in detail the Eastern idea that once upon a time creatures like but greater than men walked the earth, which is merely mentioned in *Arabia Deserta* (I, 22). It thus delves into the past more deeply than any of Doughty's other works, going beyond human history, and penetrates the future more than *The Cliffs* or *The Clouds* because of its mention of atom-splitting.

Because the Titans are superhuman monsters, the poem exceeds in spatial as well as historical imagination the scope of Doughty's other works. Despite his stated love for past artistic methods and forms, and perhaps against his intentions, the *Titans'* vast panorama has made it resemble an early film rather than a drama or a narrative poem. Its use of giants, Titans, huge reptiles, and gods affords many opportunities for sensational photography contrasting great and small size. The outlines of the horde descending on Mantown at night would make fine Disney drama, as would the battle between gods and Titans in which no human is ever hurt.

The emphasis on forces clashing rather than on individual human characters is rooted deeply in Doughty's psychology. Here we see his solitary removal from other human beings in its most naked form. In *Dawn in Britain,* he attempted through Caradoc to create a believable human character and very barely succeeded in doing so. In *The Cliffs* and *The Clouds* his characters are one-dimensional, and in *Mansoul* so vapid as not to exist. Only in *Arabia Deserta* and *Adam Cast Forth* does he manage to create sympathetic characters, but these are based on his actual experience. When he has to *imagine* people, he cannot do it, and in *The Titans* abandons the attempt totally.

The lack of human action on an individual scale makes it difficult for the reader to focus interest on this poem. Despite the moments of cartoonlike horror film excitement, too much of the poem reads like the text of a scientific documentary film which lacks any particularly beautiful or striking perceptions. Doughty is not always in control of the reader's perceptions, as when he inadvertently leads us to feel sympathy for the chained giants and Titan. His uneven style only sometimes suits the action and more frequently slides into abstract cliché: "Daughter of Heaven, adórable hóly PEACE" (106). But there are also strange, expressionistic moments reminding us of the landscapes of Max Ernst or the terrain of those who create Hollywood monster films, like this description of the inert Titans:

> Pass untold generations of Earths face:
> Whiles ivy-twine their marble knees hath knit;
> And clambering briars have wrapped about their feet:
> And stains their loins thick scab of creeping moss.
> Have swallows, in their nose-thrills, builded nests;
> And in their ear-holes, mice, ten thousand sithes.
>   (11)

In attempting in *The Titans* to press back the limits of history in past and future directions, Doughty is himself like a chained Titan who lacks the artistic and intellectual power to convince his reader. His artistic strengths in this poem (spectacular and innovative cinematic expression, and the attempt to give graphic interest to science) and weaknesses (stilted language, generalized abstract conceptions, grotesque because inhuman heroics, and a jarring mixture of technological vision and old-fashioned pastoral) are not untypical of the popular literature of his period. We see particularly clearly in this poem the Doughty who wished to transport himself elsewhere and who yet remained bound to his times. He looks forward, in *The Titans* as in all his minor poetry, without being able to envision the future spiritually rather than merely technologically, just as he looks back, in *The Dawn in Britain* and *Mansoul*, to a Gothic past that he never quite succeeded in recapturing.

CHAPTER 7

Prospect

W ILFRID Scawen Blunt, one of the first noted authors to become
aware of Doughty's work, was also the first to say that *Travels
in Arabia Deserta* constitutes "certainly the best prose written in the
last two centuries,"[1] but that Doughty's poetry was the worst of the
nineteenth century. In 1926, John Middleton Murry brilliantly
endorsed this view, with high praise for *Adam Cast Forth* added. Since
1926, critics have been divided into two camps: those who support the
Blunt-Murry assessment, perhaps with some modification, and those
who like Barker Fairley and Anne Treneer would add *The Dawn in
Britain* and other poetic works of Doughty to *Arabia Deserta* and possibly *Adam Cast Forth* as important art.

Fifty years after Doughty's death and seventy years after *Dawn*'s
publication, it must be admitted that the cause of *Dawn in Britain* and
the other poetry outside of *Adam Cast Forth* has been lost, not because
of "inexplicable" neglect, or because the poems are too long, but for
good reasons. Ezra Pound's lines sum up the situation with respect to
the bulk of Doughty's poetry:

> did we ever get to the end of Doughty:
> The Dawn in Britain?
> perhaps not
> Summons withdrawn, sir.)
> (bein' aliens in prohibited area)

These lines from Canto 83 refer to the action of the wartime British
authorities, who interrupted Pound's reading of the poem to W. B.
Yeats, but a more symbolic interpretation of this fragment reveals a
harsh truth: people begin, but rarely want to finish, reading Doughty's
poems.

And if imitation is the sincerest form of flattery, Doughty's poetry
has not been flattered. In 1957 Barker Fairley, while deploring *Dawn*'s
almost total lack of readership, could point to the fact that W. H.
162

Auden included five hundred lines of the poem in his *Poets of the English Language* (1950) and that the older G. B. Shaw "read as much Doughty as he could lay hands on."[2] We can add that Robert Bridges, John Masefield, Edward Thomas, and Hugh MacDiarmid professed admiration for Doughty's verse, and that in 1975 both Laura Riding and Guy Davenport nominated *Dawn* in a list of worthy but neglected literature which was published in the journal *Antaeus*. But these testimonials have not established the case for the merit of *Dawn* and the other poems. The truth remains that we search without result for traces of Doughty's poetry in the work of any of his poetic admirers, or in the work of Pound and Yeats for that matter. At the very most, we can point to a poem or two of MacDiarmid and Pound's poem "The Seafarer" (1912), subtitled "From the Anglo-Saxon," in which this possible pun occurs: "Delight 'mid the doughty." Guy Davenport comments about the "Renaissance of 1910" (of which Pound's poem is a part) that its "linguistic renovations . . . are still not understood, but . . . grow out of Morris' and Doughty's new sense of the genius of English."[3] This remains a very diffuse claim at best. Subsequent poets have not followed in Doughty's tracks for fear that they lead into a poetic desert.

Perhaps the strongest case for the influence—and hence the importance—of any of Doughty's poems has been made for *Adam Cast Forth*, the one poem praised by Murry and the one typically accepted by *Arabia Deserta* enthusiasts as good, if not great. Calling the poem "This shipwrecked masterpiece, which scarcely anyone reads today," Robert Payne finds signs of borrowing from it not in the poetry of Doughty's period or later, but in T. E. Lawrence's masterpiece *Seven Pillars of Wisdom:* "Lawrence seems to have known the play by heart, and sometimes it is possible to detect Doughty's rhythms in *Seven Pillars.* . . . Doughty was always at his elbow, but it was not the Doughty of *Arabia Deserta*, as wide and thunderous as the valley of Rumm, but the quieter and more lyrical Doughty of *Adam Cast Forth*."[4] The evidence for influence that he presents in his article is convincing even if we reject his claim that *Arabia Deserta* meant less artistically to Lawrence than *Adam Cast Forth.*

We can rest the case for Doughty as a poet on *Adam Cast Forth* alone. Those who like Treneer and Fairley and his followers demand recognition of *Dawn in Britain* as the superior or even equal legacy to *Arabia Deserta* put themselves in the same impossible position as a critic who would claim that Melville's reputation should rest on *Clarel* rather than on *Moby Dick*. The current American revival of the long poem has not resurrected *Dawn*. Tolkien's and not Doughty's is the epic of our times, and there is no sign that Tolkien even read Doughty, although this would appear probable in view of his Oxbridge philological background.

In recognizing and admitting the weakness of the poetry—outside of *Adam Cast Forth* and occasional passages of the rest, with *Mansoul* remaining a weak but more mellow and relaxed poem than *Dawn*[5]— we will be doing Doughty a service. Fairley's and Treneer's pressing of inflated claims for a body of work rejected by the great majority of critics over the last fifty years, and totally without influence on the poets of his generation and later, has only hurt Doughty's overall reputation, despite their superb work on *Arabia Deserta*. One reason that *Adam Cast Forth*, the one poem with some chance for recognition, is not more widely known is that it has been grouped together with the other poems by Doughty's poetic partisans, instead of fully highlighted. It is as if they would tell us to accept Doughty as "great in all his works," as Fairley puts it at the end of his study, or not at all. We can and should feel perfectly comfortable about reading *Arabia Deserta* only, with a possible allowance for *Adam Cast Forth*, and most readers and critics seem to have done just that.

Arabia Deserta's situation today remains better with general readers, academics, and artists than that of the poetry, for the good reason that it constitutes far more original, complex, and striking work. It has been praised not only by the poets who also liked Doughty's poetry, but for different reasons by Leonard Woolf, the adventurer R. B. Cunninghame Graham, F. R. Leavis, Edwin Muir, V. S. Pritchett, Herbert Read, H. M. Tomlinson, Rex Warner, Middleton Murry, Wyndham Lewis (who enjoys the book's "archaic but delightful jargon"),[6] and more recent critics. It has become part of Anglo-American culture as the poetry never has.

Even as a scientific document, *Arabia Deserta* retains some importance. Doughty was the first to record the Nabataean inscriptions at Medain Salih. He determined the correct flow of the watercourses of Wadi Hamd and Wadi er Rumma. Wilfrid Blunt testifies that Doughty's passive Christian method actually saved his life in an encounter with Arabs in North Africa.[7] In World Wars I and II British intelligence used the book as one of its primary manuals of facts about Arabia's topography and customs.

In his *Arabia of the Wahhabis*, H. St. John Philby confirms Doughty's account by recording his conversations with Arabs who remembered and respected the earlier traveler even after half a century. And the reader of R. Bayly Winder's substantial history, *Saudi Arabia in the Nineteenth Century* (1965), soon realizes that we remain indebted to Doughty almost alone for our present knowledge of the Ibn Rashid family. As Philby, one of the first Europeans to cross the Rub al Khali, or Empty Quarter, sums it up very simply in his *Encyclopedia Brittanica* article on Doughty, Doughty is "the greatest of all Arabian travellers," and *Arabia Deserta* remains the amazing record of that fact.

As literature, Doughty's book has not only been admired, but imitated. Despite Payne's interesting citation of *Adam Cast Forth*, we are far more likely to find the source of the inspiration for T. E. Lawrence's *Seven Pillars of Wisdom* in *Arabia Deserta*, as his introduction to Doughty's masterpiece, full of praise and artistic admiration, directly informs us. And the Doughty of *Arabia Deserta* is one of the very few previous travelers Lawrence mentions by name in his own book. Where but in *Arabia Deserta* will we discover how Lawrence learned to portray heroism in an epic, medieval fashion, to employ an art prose full of parallelism and archaic dialogues, fill his work with heightened color and mystery, and veil his personality (if in a different manner than Doughty)? And by reacting to whose bad example did Lawrence learn to relate to the Arabs and their culture relativistically? Since *Seven Pillars*, like *Arabia Deserta*, is a truly great book, this one case of clear influence alone establishes *Arabia Deserta*'s far-reaching importance in the Anglo-Arabian travel book tradition, which has produced some of the very best English writing. It is pointless to speculate which of the two books is the "better" (as Herbert Read has done),[8] except to say that Lawrence's will appeal to a more contemporary sensibility.

Beyond this specific case of influence, important as it is, we have the fact that Doughty's dictum "The Semites are like to a man sitting in a cloaca to the eyes and whose brows touch heaven" (which appears in *Seven Pillars'* description of the Arabs as "petty incarnate Semites who attained heights and depths beyond our reach") has passed into the English language and is cited—for better or for worse—whenever Arabs are written about, even if quotation dictionary compilers have not yet discovered this. And in an article in *Commentary* in 1960, Leslie Fiedler used it to describe the Jewish-American immigrants in Henry Roth's *Call It Sleep*.

After a slow start and an early nearly total eclipse after its initial

publication in 1888, the 330,000 word Edward Garnett abridgment
Wanderings in the Desert of 1908 and then the full edition of 1921
with Lawrence's introduction, followed by nine immediate reprints
and Garnett's 130,000 word abridgment *Passages from Arabia
Deserta* of 1931, have left *Arabia Deserta* a permanent, if unsteady,
fixture of the publishing scene in England and America.[9] During a lecture I gave on Doughty at Whittier College, Los Angeles, in 1979, I
was surprised to learn how many members of the audience were well
acquainted with his masterwork, but no more so than when the first
thing a prominent overseas visitor to the Ben-Gurion University asked
was if our library possessed a copy of the book!

Rather than the poetry's University of Toronto cult following,[10] *Arabia Deserta* enjoys appreciation at all levels of the literate audience.
The fact that it is not taught as often as it should be results primarily
from the English faculty's lack of knowledge of Near Eastern, as
opposed to European, culture. But *Arabia Deserta*'s totally original
hero, style that creates itself out of its content, complexly portrayed
interaction between Khalil and the Arab characters, the intrinsic interest of its plot, and universality that transcends Doughty's prejudices,
will ensure its continued critical strength. As the Near East becomes
ever more important to the world economy *Arabia Deserta* will experience the same revival currently enjoyed by Lawrence's work, because
both books represent one of the few ways for English-speaking literary
students to connect with this trend. The filmmakers have not yet realized that Doughty will make as good a subject as Lawrence, but the
B.B.C. featured a "Doughty" program as one of the *Ten Who Dared*
series, [11] and at least one novel based—albeit fancifully and parodisti-
cally—on his personality appeared in 1976.[12]

The time will come when *Arabia Deserta* is fully recognized for
what it is—major Victorian art prose and autobiography of a very
novel and brilliant variety—and included as such in the university
courses and anthologies that now timidly exclude it from more than a
tangential position.[13] In *Arabia Deserta* and to a lesser extent in its
coda, *Adam Cast Forth,* we find some of the very finest writing about
life's pilgrimage in any climate ever put in English or any other language. And that, surely, is all the claim we need make for any writer's
art.

Notes and References

Chapter One

1. D. G. Hogarth, *The Life of Charles M. Doughty* (London, 1928).
2. H. T. Francis's dictated remarks about Doughty to S. C. Cockerell, quoted in Hogarth, *Life*, p. 4.
3. During our conversation on 27 July 1978 from 2:30–4:15 P.M. at the Gonville and Caius Library.
4. "Die Sinai-Halbinsel," *Mitteilungen der Kaiserlich und Königlichen Geographischen Gesellschaft in Wien*, 19 (1876), 268–72.
5. Charles M. Doughty, *Travels in Arabia Deserta* (London, 1933), I, 4. This thin-paper edition contains the original two-volume work in one volume, but retains the original two-volume pagination. All subsequent references are to this edition, and quotations will be followed by volume and page number in parentheses in my text, with no other identification.
6. 37 (1880), 201; 39 (1881), 7, 23; 40 (1881), 38; 41 (1882), 214, 249.
7. 130 (August 1888), 240.
8. Charles Doughty, "Pen-Picture by Mr. Doughty," *Observer*, 19 March 1922. Privately published as *Hogarth's "Arabia"* (London, 1922).
9. June 1906, p. 107.

Chapter Two

1. In *Arabia Deserta* (II, 279) Doughty says that he kept only Sprenger and Zehme and buried all his other books. But the presence of his annotated 1876 Bible and Mrs. Robbins's catalog note that Doughty carried the book through Arabia (in the Gonville and Caius Library), seem to correct Doughty's claim. And Hogarth reproduces an annotated page of "The Reeve's Tale" in his *Life*, with the note that it comes from the "*Canterbury Tales*" which Doughty carried with him through Arabia." See Hogarth, *Life*, p. 38 for Doughty's comment that he "carried several leaves" of the *Canterbury Tales* on his journey.
2. Alois Sprenger, *Die Alte Geographie Arabiens* (Bern, 1875).

3. Richard Bevis, "Spiritual Geology: C. M. Doughty and the Land of the Arabs," *Victorian Studies*, 16, no. 2 (December 1972), 174.

4. Albrecht Zehme, *Arabien und die Araber Seit Hundert Jahren* (Halle, 1875).

5. For literary analysis of Palgrave's book, see William Rogers, "Romance, Science, and W. G. Palgrave's Central and Eastern Arabia," *Exploration*, 5, no. 2 (July 1978), 9–32.

6. For literary discussion of Kinglake, Doughty, Lawrence, and Thesiger, see my *T. E. Lawrence* (Boston, 1978). The best comprehensive histories of Arabian exploration in English are: Peter Brent, *Far Arabia* (London, 1977); Robin Fedden, "English Travellers in the Near East," Writers and their Work, no. 97 (London, 1958); D. G. Hogarth, *The Penetration of Arabia* (London, 1904); and R. H. Kiernan, *The Unveiling of Arabia* (London, 1937). Robin Bidwell's *Travellers in Arabia* (London, 1976) and Z. Freeth and H. Winstone's *Explorers of Arabia* unfortunately contribute nothing new. See also the dissertations by Rogers and Safady and the books by Assad and Nasir listed in my bibliography. There are also numerous biographies on individual travellers.

7. Hogarth, *Life*, p. 151.

8. *Academy*, 28 July 1888, p. 47.

9. (1908; reprint ed.; New York, 1966).

10. For the distinction between memoirs and autobiography, see my *T. E. Lawrence*, p. 28.

11. J. L. Burckhardt, *Travels in Arabia* (London, 1968), p. 231.

12. Ibid., p. 173.

13. T. E. Lawrence, *Men in Print* (London, 1940), p. 43.

14. Hogarth, *Life*, p. 132.

15. My dating is based on the fact that we find very little actual Hebrew in any of Doughty's works, including *Arabia Deserta*, until *Adam Cast Forth* of 1908; and that his Hebrew Bible and his S. P. Tregelles, *Hebrew Reading Lessons*, a beginner's book, were both published in 1906.

16. Annette McCormick, "Hebrew Parallelism in Doughty's *Travels in Arabia Deserta*," in *Studies in Comparative Literature*, ed. Waldo McNeir, Humanities Series, no. 11 (Baton Rouge, 1962), pp. 29–46. McCormick errs when she writes "Nor have I found evidence that he read ancient Hebrew" (p. 32) but her error does not affect her argument since, as I have shown in the preceding footnote, he probably learned that language only *after* he wrote *Arabia Deserta*.

17. Walt Taylor, "Doughty's English," Society for Pure English, Tract no. 11 (Oxford, 1939).

18. Annette McCormick, "An Elizabethan-Victorian Travel Book: Doughty's *Travels in Arabia Deserta*," in *Essays in Honor of Esmond Linworth Marilla*, ed. Thomas Kirby and William Olive (Baton Rouge, 1970), pp. 230–42.

19. William Rogers, "Arabian Involvement: A Study of Five Victorian

Travel Narratives" (Ph.D. diss., University of California at Berkeley, 1971), pp. 183–84.

20. John Dixon Hunt, *The Pre-Raphaelite Imagination 1848–1900* (Lincoln, Nebraska, 1968), pp. 2, 23, 30.

21. Hugh Kenner, *The Pound Era* (Berkeley, 1971), p. 108.

22. Information courtesy of Mrs. Robbins.

23. See Lawrence's letter of 30 July 1920 quoted in my next chapter.

24. Doughty's letter to Cockerell of 26 March 1909, quoted in Hogarth, *Life*, p. 52.

25. *The Penetration of Arabia*, p. 275.

26. 10 January 1884 to Bates, quoted in Hogarth, *Life*, p. 109.

27. This and the other Saunders letters are in the Gonville and Caius Library.

28. Barker Fairley, *Charles M. Doughty* (London, 1927), p. 30.

29. D. H. Lawrence, *Studies in Classic American Literature* (New York, 1966), p. 146.

30. William Howarth, "Some Principles of Autobiography," *New Literary History* (Winter 1974), 363–81. For the application of Howarth's principles to T. E. Lawrence and a model of autobiographical elements, see my *T. E. Lawrence*, pp. 28–30, 116–18.

31. Joseph Conrad, *Conrad's Prefaces to His Works*, ed. Edward Garnett (New York, 1971), p. 52.

32. But see Annette McCormick, "The Origins and Development of the Styles of Charles M. Doughty's *Arabia Deserta*" (Ph.D. diss., Bedford College, University of London, 1952), for a different viewpoint. See my *T. E. Lawrence*, pp. 129–36, for an analysis of Lawrence's styles.

33. Hogarth, *Life*, p. 132.

Chapter Three

1. Brent, *Far Arabia*, p. 85.

2. Dated 30 July 1920; in the Gonville and Caius Library.

3. Letter of 1902 to Hogarth, quoted in *Life*, p. 114.

4. Stanley Fish, *Self-Consuming Artifacts* (Berkeley, 1972), p. 3.

5. Jonathan Bishop, "The Heroic Ideal in Doughty's *Arabia Deserta*," *Modern Language Quarterly*, 21 (1960), 59–68.

6. Richard Burton, "Mr. Doughty's Travels," *Academy* 34 (28 July 1888), 48.

7. Thomas J. Assad, *Three Victorian Travellers* (London, 1964), pp. 124; 130–31.

8. A. H. S., "Travels in Arabia Deserta," *Nature*, 38 (28 June 1888), 195.

9. Quoted in Hogarth, *Life*, p. 95.

10. Norman Douglas, "Arabia Deserta," *London Mercury*, 4, no. 19 (May 1921), 67.

Chapter Four

1. Fairley, *Charles M. Doughty*, p. 41.

Chapter Five

1. Charles Doughty, *Mansoul* (London, 1923), pp. 225–26. All references are to this edition.
2. Fairley, *Charles Doughty*, p. 93.
3. J. Middleton Murry, "Charles Montagu Doughty," *Times Literary Supplement*, 11 February 1926, p. 86.
4. John Holloway, "Poetry and Plain Language: The Verse of C. M. Doughty," *Essays in Criticism*, 4, no. 1 (January 1954), 64–65.
5. Charles Doughty, *The Dawn in Britain*, introduction by Ruth M. Robbins (London, 1943), p. 682. All references are to this edition.
6. Doughty, *Dawn in Britain*, p. 207.
7. See Barker Fairley, "The *Dawn in Britain* after Fifty Years," *University of Toronto Quarterly*, 26, no. 2 (1957), p. 161, and John Heath-Stubbs, *The Darkling Plain* (London, 1950), p. 198.
8. Charles Doughty, *The Cliffs* (London, 1909), p. 41. All references are to this edition.
9. Anonymous, "An Epic of Britain," *Times Literary Supplement*, 20 April 1906, p. 140.
10. T. E. Lawrence, *The Letters of T. E. Lawrence*, ed. David Garnett (London, 1938), p. 438.
11. Murry, "Charles Montagu Doughty," p. 85.
12. *The Darkling Plain*, p. 192.
13. John Ruskin, *The Stones of Venice*, ed. J. G. Links (New York, 1960), p. 160.
14. Ibid., p. 161.
15. Ibid., p. 169.
16. Ibid., p. 173.
17. Ibid., p. 174.
18. Herman Melville, *Clarel*, ed. Walter Bezanson (New York, 1960), p. lxv.
19. Samuel Chew, "Other Late Victorian Poets: Doughty," in *A Literary History of England*, ed. Albert Baugh (Boston, 1967), p. 1541.
20. Anne Treneer, *Charles M. Doughty* (London, 1938), p. 191.
21. Charles Doughty, *Adam Cast Forth: A Sacred Drama in Five Songs* (London, 1908), second page after title page. All references are to this edition.
22. Murry "Charles Montagu Doughty," p. 85.
23. *Mansoul*, p. 3.
24. Holloway, "Poetry and Plain Language," p. 69.

Chapter Six

1. Advertisement for *The Cliffs* and *The Clouds* on the back cover of Charles Doughty, *The Titans* (London, 1916).
2. Doughty, *The Cliffs*, p. 54.
3. Murry, "Charles Montagu Doughty," p. 85.
4. 10 June 1927; in the British Library.
5. Charles Doughty, *The Clouds* (London, 1912), p. 94. All references are to this edition.
6. Samuel Chew, "The Poetry of Charles Montague Doughty," *North American Review*, 222 (December–February 1925–26), 297.
7. Charles Doughty, *The Titans* (London, 1916), p. 9. All references are to this edition.

Chapter Seven

1. Wilfrid Blunt, *My Diaries* (London, 1932), p. 273. For Blunt's view of the poetry, see Edith Finch, *Wilfrid Scawen Blunt 1840–1922* (London, 1938), p. 338.
2. Barker Fairley, "*The Dawn in Britain* after Fifty Years," *University of Toronto Quarterly*, 26, no. 2 (1957), 163. But for Shaw's wickedly brilliant opinion of *Arabia Deserta*, see *The Best of Friends: Further Letters to S. C. Cockerell*, ed. V. Meynell (London, 1956), pp. 140–41.
3. Guy Davenport, "Persephone's Ezra," in *New Approaches to Ezra Pound*, ed. Eva Hesse (Berkeley, 1969), p. 150.
4. Robert Payne, "On the Prose of T. E. Lawrence," *Prose*, 4 (Spring 1972), 103–4.
5. The compilers of *Books for College Libraries*, ed. Melvin Voight and Joseph Tregg (Chicago, 1967), seem to support this assessment. Their list of essential college library purchases includes only *Arabia Deserta, Adam Cast Forth,* and *Mansoul* among Doughty's works. This prompted Scholarly Reprints to reissue *Mansoul* in 1971 and AMS Press to reprint *Adam Cast Forth* in 1976. Unfortunately, *Adam* has sold "very poorly" as Dr. William B. Long, AMS Editor, wrote me on 8 May 1979. And *Mansoul* is now out of print again. However, the reissue of Fairley's, Hogarth's, and Taylor's works on Doughty by reprint houses during the last ten years testifies to a possible Doughty revival.
6. Wyndham Lewis, *Blasting and Bombardiering* (Berkeley, 1967), p. 242.
7. Blunt, *My Diaries*, p. 273.
8. See Herbert Read, "Lawrence of Arabia," in *A Coat of Many Colours: Occasional Essays* (London, 1945), pp. 19–26.
9. At least five editions have appeared in England and America since

1931. But a letter of 17 May 1979 from Donald S. Klopfer of Random House to me clarifies the book's publishing situation even today: "From memory, we did several editions of the book. The first one in two volumes and then we did a one-volume edition. I don't know whether they were ever reprinted and I am sure that the original printing was no greater than two or three thousand. . . . It's a great book, but we couldn't sell enough copies to keep it in print." Peter Smith and Dover are *Arabia Deserta*'s latest American publishers.

The book's British publishing history is not that much different, as a letter of 7 June 1979 from Jonathan Cape's Graham C. Greene to me indicates: " . . . we appear to have kept *Travels* continuously in print between publication in 1921 and its going out of print in 1971 apart from a gap of a few years in the late thirties/early forties which may however be a gap in our records rather than in the printing history. Very approximately, in the fifty years of publication we sold 21,000 copies. We do not have any immediate plans to reissue. . . . You also ask about *Dawn in Britain* and the Garnett abridgement of *Travels*. We published the first in a very small edition in 1943, sold it out within a year and did not reprint. The Garnett edition of *Travels* went out of print not long after the complete edition in 1972 and, sadly, for the same reason: there is always tremendous interest in Doughty but the annual sales dropped off considerably in the last few years of publication."

10. But there are defectors from the Toronto camp. Douglas Grant's illuminating "Barker Fairley on Charles Doughty," *University of Toronto Quarterly*, 36, no. 3 (1967), 220–28, explains why Fairley liked the poetry and why most other critics—including Grant—cannot follow him on this however much they praise *Arabia Deserta*.

11. For the program's script in book form, see Desmond Wilcox, *Ten Who Dared* (Boston, 1977).

12. My privately-published *Through the Gate of Tears* (Jerusalem, 1976). Available at major libraries in America, England, and Israel.

13. To which it has been relegated, at least in England, by F. R. Leavis's kiss-of-death praise: "it will remain a respected but little-read minor classic." See "Doughty and Hopkins," *Scrutiny*, 4, no. 3 (December 1935), 317.

Selected Bibliography

PRIMARY SOURCES

1. Manuscript Collections
   British Library.
   Fitzwilliam Museum, Cambridge.
   Gonville and Caius College Library, Cambridge.

2. Major Works
Adam Cast Forth: A Sacred Drama in Five Songs. London: Duckworth, 1908.
The Cliffs: A Drama of the Time, in Five Parts. London: Duckworth, 1909.
The Clouds. London: Duckworth, 1912.
The Dawn in Britain. Introduction by Ruth M. Robbins. London: Jonathan Cape, 1943.
Documents épigraphiques recueillis dans le nord de l'Arabie. Edited by Ernest Renan. Paris: Académie des Inscriptions et Belles Lettres, 1884.
Hogarth's "Arabia." London: Privately printed, 1922.
Mansoul or The Riddle of the World. London: Selwyn and Blount, 1920.
Mansoul or The Riddle of the World. Rev. ed. London: Jonathan Cape and the Medici Society, 1923.
On the Jöstedal-brae Glaciers in Norway. London: Edward Stanford, 1866.
Passages from Arabia Deserta. Selected by Edward Garnett. London: Jonathan Cape, 1931.
Selected Passages from "The Dawn in Britain" of Charles Doughty. Arranged with an Introduction by Barker Fairley. London: Duckworth, 1935.
The Titans. London: Duckworth, 1916.
Travels in Arabia Deserta. Introduction by T. E. Lawrence. London: Jonathan Cape, 1933.
Under Arms 1900. London: Printed by the Army and Navy Co-operative Society, 1900
Wanderings in Arabia. Edited by Edward Garnett. 2 vols. London: Duckworth, 1908.

SECONDARY SOURCES

1. Books

ASSAD, THOMAS J. *Three Victorian Travellers: Burton, Blunt, Doughty.* London: Routledge and Kegan Paul, 1964. Lucid, well-researched analysis of Doughty's attitudes toward the Arabs in the context of his period.

FAIRLEY, BARKER. *Charles M. Doughty: A Critical Study.* London: Jonathan Cape, 1927. Pioneering literary analysis of Doughty's work and still one of the most astute readings of *Arabia Deserta,* but greatly overvalues the poetry, especially *Dawn,* unconvincingly insisting that we see Doughty as "great in all his works."

HOGARTH, DAVID G. *The Life of Charles M. Doughty.* London: Oxford University Press, 1928. Highly reliable and contains superb work on the *Arabia Deserta* notebooks, but neglects the inner man.

TRENEER, ANNE. *Charles M. Doughty: A Study of his Prose and Verse.* London: Jonathan Cape, 1938. Overestimates the poetry like Fairley, but provides a sensitive interpretation of all the works emphasizing Doughty's individual word choice.

2. Literary articles, dissertations, and parts of books

ANON. "Doughty as an Influence Today: An Over-Simple Creed." *Times Literary Supplement,* 9 November 1935, p. 716. Penetrating criticism of Doughty's poetry and Fairley's and Treneer's praise of it.

BEVIS, RICHARD. "Spiritual Geology: C. M. Doughty and the Land of the Arabs." *Victorian Studies,* 16, no. 2 (December 1972), 163–81. The influence of Doughty's geological studies on his outlook and motivation for Arabian travels.

BISHOP, JONATHAN. "The Heroic Ideal in Doughty's *Arabia Deserta.*" *Modern Language Quarterly,* 21, no. 1 (March 1960), 59–68. Argues that Doughty's passive resistance is a reversal of the usual Victorian heroic ideal.

BURTON, RICHARD FRANCIS. "Mr. Doughty's Travels in Arabia." *The Academy,* 34, no. 847 (28 July 1888), 47–48. Pointed contemporary criticism by a rival.

CHEW, SAMUEL. "The Poetry of Charles Montague Doughty." *North American Review* 222, no. 829 (December–February 1925–1926), 287–98. Generally uncritical praise of all Doughty's work including even "the chant of the Sacred Band" which closes *The Cliffs,* but interesting as an example of what Doughty's contemporary poetic admirers liked in his work.

DAVIS, HERBERT. "Charles Doughty 1843–1926." Bergen Lecture, Yale University, 23 November 1943. *Aurora VII.* New York: Wells College Press, 1945. Centennial overview stressing the relation of Doughty's poetry to World War II.

FAIRLEY, BARKER. "Charles Doughty and Modern Poetry." *London Mercury*, 32, no. 188 (June 1935), 128–37. Argues for similarity between poetry of Hopkins, MacDiarmid, and Doughty.

———. "Charles Doughty (1843–1926)." *University of Toronto Quarterly*, 13, no. 1 (1943), 14–24. Centennial overview stressing relation of Doughty's work to England at war.

———. "*The Dawn in Britain* after Fifty Years." *University of Toronto Quarterly* 26, no. 2 (1957), 149–65. Attempts to defend the poem's structure and quality against attacks.

GRANT, DOUGLAS. "Barker Fairley on Charles Doughty." *University of Toronto Quarterly* 26, no. 3 (1967), 220–28. Explains and intelligently disagrees with Fairley's adulation of Doughty's poetry.

HEATH-STUBBS, JOHN. *The Darkling Plain*. London: Eyre and Spottiswoode, 1950. Pp. 188–99. "The best account" of *Dawn in Britain* "that we have" according to Fairley, but all readers may not agree that Heath-Stubbs convinces them of Doughty's success in recapturing the spirit of past ages, because he overlooks the poem's failures.

HOLLOWAY, JOHN. "Poetry and Plain Language: The Verse of C. M. Doughty." *Essays in Criticism*, 4, no. 1 (January 1954), 58–70. Argues that *Dawn in Britain*'s epic style is a "narrow success," although the poem's structure and characterization are weak.

JACKSON, LAURA RIDING. "The 'Right English' of Charles M. Doughty." *University of Toronto Quarterly* 46, no. 4 (1977), 309–21. Laura Riding's account of her husband's philological work on *Dawn in Britain* concludes with his interlinear "translation" of some lines of the poem into the modern English against which all of Doughty's work is an explicit protest. Some readers may find themselves preferring Jackson's translation to Doughty's original.

LEAVIS, F. R. "Doughty and Hopkins." *Scrutiny*, 4, no. 3 (December 1935), 316–17. Flatly rejects Fairley's and Treneer's claims of the importance of Doughty's poetry, places Doughty outside the "great tradition," but finds *Arabia Deserta* a "minor classic."

MCCORMICK, ANNETTE. "An Elizabethan-Victorian Travel Book: Doughty's Travels in Arabia Deserta." In *Essays in Honor of Esmond Linworth Marilla*, edited by Thomas Kirby and William Olive, pp. 230–42. Baton Rouge: Louisiana State University Press, 1970. Disappointing attempt to show influence of Elizabethan travel books on *Arabia Deserta*.

———. "Hebrew Parallelism in Doughty's *Travels in Arabia Deserta*." *Studies in Comparative Literature*. Humanities Series, no. 11. Edited by Waldo McNeir. Baton Rouge: Louisiana State University Press, 1962, pp. 29–46. Demonstrates the important influence of English Bible translations on Doughty's style in *Arabia Deserta*.

MURRY, JOHN MIDDLETON. "Charles Montagu Doughty." *Times Literary Sup-*

plement, 11 February 1926, pp. 85–86. Slightly exaggerated both positively and negatively, but still the clearest and most brilliant view of Doughty's total strengths and weaknesses to date.

————. *"Arabia Deserta." The Adelphi*, 3 (March 1926), 657–65. " . . . Doughty was much rather the writer of one great book than a great writer."

NASIR, SARI J. *The Arabs and the English*. London: Longman, 1976. This comprehensive survey contains much excellent research on British attitudes toward the Arabs as expressed in literature and film. Although a more valuable work of scholarship than Said's *Orientalism*, it too presents a partisan viewpoint and must therefore be treated with caution. More objective recent histories of the Anglo-Arabian literary tradition are Thomas Assad's *Three Victorian Travellers* and Peter Brent's *Far Arabia*.

ROGERS, WILLIAM N. "Arabian Involvement: A Study of Five Victorian Travel Narratives." Ph.D. dissertation, University of California at Berkeley, 1971. A lucid study of the literary sensibilities of Doughty and his Anglo-Arabian predecessors.

————, and TABACHNICK, S. E. "British Literary Responses to the Near East: C. M. Doughty and T. E. Lawrence." Taped one-hour colloquium. San Diego State University, 18 April 1979. Doughty by W. Rogers; Lawrence by S. Tabachnick. Rogers compares *Arabia Deserta*'s style with the prose of some of Doughty's contemporaries, and puts him in the context of nineteenth-century Anglo-Arabian travelers.

SAFADY, ISSAM. "Attempt and Attainment: A Study of Some Literary Aspects of Charles Doughty's *Arabia Deserta* as the Culmination of Late-Victorian Anglo-Arabian Travel Books to the Levant." Ph.D. dissertation, University of Kentucky, 1968. Written under the supervision of Doughty enthusiast Guy Davenport, this dissertation presents Doughty's book as "not about the land he visited but *of* it."

SAID, EDWARD. *Orientalism*. New York: Pantheon, 1978. Said's scattered remarks on Doughty and T. E. Lawrence totally ignore almost all important recent and older work on these writers and suffer from superficiality as a result. But he presents some insights into their contribution to Western stereotypes of the Arabs in the context of a shrill and biased polemic against Western "Oriental" scholarship.

STORRS, RONALD. "The Spell of Arabia: Charles Doughty and T. E. Lawrence." *Listener*, 38 (25 December 1947), 1093–94. " . . . who shall ever set down all the subconscious thoughts and dreams that impelled these great Pilgrims to make their Progress in Arabia?"

TABACHNICK, STEPHEN E. "Adam Cast Forth: The First Sentence of Doughty's *Arabia Deserta." The Pre-Raphaelite Review*, 1, no. 2 (May 1978), 49–63. Partially included in this book.

TABACHNICK, STEPHEN E. *T. E. Lawrence*. Boston: Twayne, G. K. Hall, 1978. Pp. 41–45, 87–91. Doughty and Lawrence compared as writers and travellers.

——. "Two 'Arabian' Romantics: Charles Doughty and T. E. Lawrence." *English Literature in Transition: 1880–1920*, 16, no. 1 (1973), 11–25. Influence of Doughty on Lawrence spiritually and artistically.

TAYLOR, WALT. "Doughty's English." S. P. E. Tract, no. 11. Oxford: Clarendon Press, 1939. Brilliant forty-one page study of the influence of Arabic on Doughty's English, and the etymology of his older English words. Indispensable.

TUCKER, JOHN A. "A Study Towards an Edition of *The Dawn in Britain* by Charles M. Doughty." Ph.D. dissertation, University of Toronto, 1975. Attempts to argue for the poem's originality and historical accuracy.

Index